Trains, Planes and Computers

Trains, Planes and Computers

FROM EXECUTIVE JET TO BUS PASS

Stan Price

ISBN, paperback: 978-1-80227-125-6
ISBN, ebook: 978-1-80227-126-3

This book is typeset in Perpetua

Dedicated to my darling Rosemary

CONTENTS

INTRODUCTION

Although I have rarely kept a diary documenting what one has done comes naturally to a person such as myself, who, for a number of years, was a computer programmer.

This is especially necessary if what one is documenting is somewhat unique. Even more so, if what one is describing is of historical interest and is not coherently documented elsewhere. I believe this to be the case with the UK's acquisition of the US's computer system for air traffic control with which I was significantly involved. Also, I believe with some justification that I can claim that my life, and especially my career, has included a number of other unique situations, although not of the general historical interest of the air traffic control situation. These include:

- Being one of the first in the world to have the job title, software engineer.
- Conceiving what later came to be called a computer database.
- Developing a modus operandi for monitoring collaborative research projects.
- Implementing a way of teaching software development via student teams working on real life projects.

However, perhaps the most unique feature of my career and also outside interests is my involvement in an unusually wide spread of sectors of society, including:

- Working in a large engineering company.
- Working in a medium-sized enterprise.
- Working in and with several disparate civil service organisations.
- Setting up and working in one's own small limited company.
- Teaching and being involved in research in academia.
- Being an expert witness in the legal system.
- Holding positions in the Church.
- Being active in community protest groups.

The breadth of my experience, although primarily in the UK, has included a US and a European dimension. Therefore, I have a breadth of experience denied to those who have worked all their lives in one profession and location, and I can identify issues that are both common and different across society.

Documenting these experiences aside, writing an autobiography also implies an arrogant assumption that other people would be interested in one's life and experiences. If it is arrogance, my justification for writing my autobiography is based on the active encouragement of many relatives, friends and acquaintances, and the more passive one that people are usually very receptive to my many anecdotes.

I therefore hope this autobiography is of interest generally and must express my thanks to the many who have helped me, both overall and in the specific compilation of this autobiography.

Rosemary – The best thing that ever happened to me.

Stan Price

CHAPTER 1

CHILDHOOD

I was not only a wartime baby but also a result of the Second World War. My parents apparently were not disposed towards marriage until my father's home in Salford was blitzed, and he came to live with my mother's family. Then, because of the prevalent social mores of the time, they decided to get married.

Although both were working class, my mother had attended a grammar school until the family's financial circumstances, cost of books, etc, forced her to leave early and get a job. It is therefore probable that she saw fulfilment for what she had missed through her sons. However, her desires were never imposed on them in any domineering way. Her character, in fact, was entirely the opposite in that she was always willing to see good in and accommodate others, only displaying steel when her family was concerned.

Mother, Alice, was tall, black-haired, slender and beautiful, whereas Father, Tom, was short, stout and bald. He was more forceful than Mother but ruthlessly honest, a quality which he drummed into me and stayed with me for the rest of my life. However, I cannot say I always lived up to this ideal, as later chapters will reveal. Although, never having a lot of money, he also abhorred debt, despite in his early years being given a glimpse of the high life whilst working as a chauffeur to a rich family on Anglesey. Old photographs almost always showed him smartly dressed: trilby on his head; binoculars round his neck leaning on the white rails of some racecourse or another. His nickname amongst his contemporaries was "Posh Price".

I could not have asked for better parents, and their influence on me in my formative years no doubt has led to a possibly over-perfectionist view of human relations.

Alice and Tom – My Parents.

I never knew my grandparents. The death of the last surviving one, my maternal grandmother Rose, having been expedited by the shock of the Blitz. However, the family home at 91 Hazelbottom Road was full for some years after I was born. For a time, two of my father's younger brothers, home from army service in the Far East and Europe, were in residence. Longer-term, my father's younger sister lived with us before leaving for a rather unsatisfactory marriage. Aunt Bessie was meek and mild, unlike the other long term resident Aunt Nellie, my mother's elder sister.

Nellie was a pillar of the local church, Saint Thomas's, supervisor at the CWS Biscuit Factory down the road, and rather a harridan. Nevertheless, she had one redeeming factor, as far as I was concerned: she doted on me. However, the presence of the aunts, particularly Nellie, was rather hard on my mother and a source of irritation with my father. Nellie's departure, therefore, had to be contrived. My mother's brother-in-law, Uncle Jack, worked for British Railways in Westbury Wiltshire and, in cahoots with my father, arranged an introduction for Nellie to a recently widowed engine driver. Fortunately, romance blossomed although, at the last minute, Nellie got cold feet, and it is reported had to be manhandled onto the train at London Road (now Piccadilly) Station. Even more fortunately, the marriage was a happy one, and Nellie grew plumper and more even-tempered, which my father put down to regular sex.

Living with this cohort of women possibly influenced me significantly, and indeed, my partner in later life, Rosemary, always ascribed my idiosyncrasies to "the aunts".

Prior to this, the traces of war had slowly disappeared, including the Anderson air-raid shelter in the back garden and the anti-aircraft guns in the field opposite number 91. One wartime incident that my mother often recounted was three German prisoners from the prisoner-of-war camp on the sports field behind 91, being invited into our home at Christmas or New Year's Eve and one crying as he recalled his own family back home. Sadly, I no longer have the wooden toys the prisoners made for me.

Between Nellie's departure and then Bessie's, also to get married, my only sibling, John, was born. He was a constantly happy child, though his spell of hospitalisation after he was born meant I had to have school dinners, which did not endear him to me. Also, his penchant for increasing the gauge of the track of my model railway by walking on it was not conducive to brotherly love.

Hazelbottom Road ran north-south in the valley of the River Irk, two miles north of Manchester City Centre. Although technically a couple of hundred yards outside its boundary, we were part of the village of Lower Crumpsall. Dominating the village was the Cooperative Wholesale Society (CWS) Biscuit Factory making the famous Crumpsall Cream Crackers. The village had terraced houses on side streets off the continuation of Hazelbottom Road and shops, including a haberdasher, a chippie, and a greengrocer. There were also three pubs. Beside the river was a children's playground with swings and slides. There was a Methodist Chapel and the parish church, Saint Thomas's, with its associated primary school alongside.

The village was also characterised by vile smells, which emanated from the Imperial Chemical Industry's (ICI) dye works to the north. The works was also responsible for the pollution of the river, which caused it to be a different vivid colour each day. The ICI works had been considerably expanded during World War One when it was discovered that the UK was dependant on the German chemical industry. Along with the expansion of the works, houses for the workers, including the chemists, had been constructed in 1919, and 91 was one of these, with my parents renting it from ICI.

To the rear of 91 was the private sports ground for ICI employees, including cricket and soccer pitches, a bowling green and four tennis courts.

The locale was also noted for its comedians, and Les Dawson was born locally and married at Saint Thomas's.

From an early age, I was a prodigious reader and once a week walked the mile or so to the local library on Cheetham Hill, returning and then collecting eight books. Amongst my favourites were the Captain W.E. Johns *Biggles* adventures and Richmal Crompton's *William* stories. We had no television, but I regularly listened to the radio. One specific recollection is the broadcasting of Galsworthy's *The Forsyte Saga* with the Enigma Variations as the theme music. This introduced me to classical music and a lifetime fondness for the works of Elgar.

My early life was not just confined to the immediate area around Lower Crumpsall; on Sundays, we regularly went by bus and train to visit my mother's elder sister, Aunt Emily, and family. They lived in Higher Poynton in Cheshire on the edge of Lyme Park, which later became famous for the set of a version of Pride and Prejudice.

The trip to Higher Poynton involved taking a number 53 bus (which, first as a tram and then a bus was a Manchester legend) around the then Manchester Ring Road. It was also the route my father used to take me to watch Belle Vue Rangers Rugby League Team, previously Broughton Rangers, which he had supported as a boy. Both involved passing Bradford Colliery, which was located amazingly only a mile from Manchester City Centre. The winding gear of the colliery and the overhead cranes at the nearby Richard Johnson and Nephew wire works fascinated me, and I faithfully replicated them in my Meccano set.

Visiting Aunt Emily's house was rather like stepping back in time in that it had no electric lighting, only gas, and the toilet was outdoors. Emily had four children, my considerably elder cousins; three boys and one girl. When the girl, Hilda, got married, I was one of the pageboys, and much against my wishes, I had to wear a silk outfit with shiny buckled shoes.

A much more interesting memory was the visit to the AVRO aircraft factory at Woodford, Cheshire, where my eldest cousin, Albert, worked. Woodford was manufacturing the Vulcan bomber at the time. The three production lines of that remarkable delta-winged aircraft left an indelible impression on me, and it was where I was later to work.

Another visit to relatives, which I remembered because it was the only time I met them, was to distant cousins on my mother's side in York who interestingly ran a company which manufactured church organs etc.

Otherwise, apart from holidays, my travels were confined to trips with the wolf cubs, train spotting outings, Manchester City away matches and accompanying my father at work. The former introduced me to the delights of the Peak District. Although generally pleasant, they could also be taxing. On one occasion, after getting soaked on Kinder Scout, I was forced to cower, stripped to my underpants, before the fire in the waiting room on Hayfield Station, whilst my clothes dried.

Some years later, another memorable hike was the two-day one for my Boy Scouts first class badge. Along with a companion, John Repton, we set off from Greenfield in rapidly deteriorating winter weather over to Arnfield. We spent the night in a small tent listening to the wind and rain whilst our parents, who had received reports of the conditions, worried.

The train spotting trips took me further and further afield. Initially, just in the Manchester Area to the main stations and the locomotive depots at Newton Heath (my second home), Longsight and Trafford Park. Then to Crewe, Leeds and then further afield still - Carlisle and even Perth in Scotland.

45700 Amethyst – A member of my favourite class of locomotives, Jubilees, and one shedded at Newton Heath.

One trip that combined train spotting with a City away game was against Tottenham Hotspur at White Hart Lane in London at Easter 1960. It also led me to meeting my first girlfriend, with white high-heeled shoes and fourteen petticoats on the train trip south. She helped the train spotting by copying engine numbers down as I shouted them out, passing Derby Locomotive Works and Shed.

It was also my first entrepreneurial venture. I took a photograph of Britannia Class Locomotive 70038, Robin Hood at Liverpool Street Station and afterwards sold prints to the Manchester spotters to whom the locomotive was a rarity.

Sold for six old pennies.

Incidentally, City won by the only goal scored by their centre-forward, Billy McAdams, in the second half, despite Denis Law limping on the wing. The match was also interesting in that Spurs were awarded a penalty in the last minute of the first half. It was taken by Cliff Jones and was parried by the legendary City goalkeeper Bert Trautman. Jones netted the rebound, but by then, the Referee had blown for half-time, so it was no goal.

Another sporting memory was lying on the grass at Old Trafford Cricket Ground and watching Jim Laker take 19 Australian wickets during the 1956 Ashes series. Old Trafford was where, two years earlier, as the winner of an Eagle comic competition, I met the England team.

For the first few years of my life, the family holidays were taken in the Isle of Man with the excitement of the ferry trip from either Liverpool or Fleetwood to Douglas. One, however, was through a severe gale, and I can still remember being violently seasick on my father's knee, watching the waves roll past an opposite porthole. Later holidays were in Bournemouth travelling via the Pines Express from Manchester London Road, now Piccadilly Station, with silver service lunch in the restaurant car.

Later holidays were also generally via the Pines Express but changing stations in Bath in order to reach Westbury, where Auntie Nellie now lived. It was also the home of my Uncle Jack and Aunt Bertha. We normally stayed there for two weeks taking day trips to Bournemouth and Weymouth by charabanc. I, of course, used these holidays to further my train spotting experiences by travelling to places such as Salisbury, Southampton, Exeter and Bristol, particularly as I grew older and was entrusted to holiday on my own. However, I was about eleven when I had a bout of homesickness and returned to Manchester before my parents and brother John could join me. I could not be certain, but a factor may have been the disputes I had with the local trainspotters over my northern accent in the fields near Westbury, alongside the main London Paddington to Devon and Cornwall railway line.

My father's work consisted of delivering ironmongery from a warehouse in Trafford Park, Manchester, around South East Lancashire, including Bury, Bolton and Rochdale. Not only did accompanying increase the bonding between us, but it informed me about the concept of foreigners and the black economy. This is where Father transported goods between points on his rounds which were not part of his employer's load, for cash in hand payments. The characters at Father's points of call now seem to me somewhat Damon Runeyonesque, except a Lancashire version. They included the widow of Tottington and Ken, the wire worker of Bolton.

I was fourteen when I first ventured abroad via a school trip to Paris for which my mother scrimped and saved. We travelled by Newhaven to Dieppe by ferry, having first taken the night train to London, which I thus saw for the first time. Paris also gave me the opportunity to sample alcohol for about the second time, the first being a pint of bitter in a pub, the Millstone Grit adjacent to my home. My French poison was Dubonnet, and I learnt a valuable French lesson when, instead of using "encore", I asked for "un autre", implying the first needed to be replaced because it was unsatisfactory.

Despite the family's relative poverty, my parents saw that my brother and I never went without food, which my mother excellently cooked, despite the wartime rationing which persisted until the 1950s. The ration allowance, as with many families, was augmented via the black market. A particular item of note was large succulent gammon steaks provided by a friend of my father's who worked for a wholesale butcher and whom we christened the Gammon King.

My childhood was generally very happy except as a foretaste of things to come when formal education interfered with my reading, train spotting, etc. The only other significant negative was I was relatively unhealthy and lacking in sporting ability, which led to a little bullying. However, I put a stop to that with a fight in the primary school playground, which left one of my persecutors somewhat bloodied.

Stan Price

CHAPTER 2

SCHOOLDAYS

I was five when I started at Saint Thomas's County Primary. Although the school was only some three hundred yards along Hazelbottom Road, the journey on my first morning took around quarter of an hour because I frequently sat down on the payment bawling that I did not want to go on.

However, I soon settled down. At Saint Thomas's, I later realised that although my family was working class both in financial terms and generally, we were slightly higher in the social pecking order than some of my schoolmates' families. One manifestation of this was I regularly was infested with fleas, and on one occasion, ringworm, transferred from a particularly unhygienic kid who sat next to me.

It was over a year at St Thomas's before the sixes teacher, a Miss or Mrs Butterworth, noted I was particularly bright and thereafter was particularly favoured by my teachers. The attentions of one teacher, a bachelor, were particularly unwelcome on one occasion. Along with one or two of his other pupils, he organised us attending a learned society's meetings, and on one occasion, I was conscious he was undoing my flies in a cloakroom. That was the only occasion, and, apart from it sticking in my memory, I am not conscious of it having any long-term effect on me.

Saint Thomas's was located across the road from the Biscuit Factory. The mainly female workforce every Friday were presented with large bags of broken biscuits, and the St Thomas pupils used to pester them, asking, "Could I have your broken biscuits, misses?"

My academic prowess meant I took the eleven-plus examination, which determined whether I would go to an elite grammar school, a technical school, or a secondary modern, a year earlier than was normal. I duly passed for the local grammar school, North Manchester, but I also had been entered for several of the local, independent grammars, including the prestigious Manchester Grammar and Chethams.

Chethams, at the time, was not the centre of musical excellence it was later to become but was the collegiate college for Manchester Cathedral. Having passed the entrance examination for the latter but not the former, my parents sent me there.

For reasons I have never been able to satisfactorily determine, I took a disliking to Chethams, and even though my parents started to escort me there each morning, I would find a way of escaping. This went on for some months and resulted in me walking miles, including down into Cheshire.

After three months, Chethams decided that they had had enough of me, so I was sent to North Manchester. Unabashed, I persisted with my truancy until finally I was sent to the local secondary modern, Domatt Street. It has been suggested that the reason for my behaviour was that I was missing my primary school friends, all of whom bar one girl had gone to secondary moderns. I do not think this was the reason, and a hint as to the reason has only been suggested to me in recent years. My cub mistress at the time, Joan Hindley, said I had referred to the spooky nature of Chetham's medieval buildings and maybe my vivid imagination had taken over. Whatever the reason, the whole episode was naturally of great concern to my parents. It resulted in the only occasion when my mother resorted to corporal punishment – taking a cane to me – which she ever after regretted.

Naturally, I academically shone at Domatt Street and was awarded a First Prize for Excellence in the Cadbury National Essay Writing Competition for Schools.

I was then again entered for the following year's eleven plus, for which, of course, I was still eligible. Incidentally, I quite enjoyed the eleven plus as the logical questions suited my particular penchant for mental gymnastics. Not surprisingly, I again passed and started the next academic year at North Manchester. This time there were no shenanigans, and in the examinations at the end of the first term, I was top of my form. Thereafter, I was permanently in the top stream of what was a very good grammar school, culminating in my receiving the Sixth Form Prize in my final year.

An indication of the academic success of North Manchester Grammar was that half of the annual intake of approximately 120 pupils, mainly working-class, went on to University at a time when only less than 5% of the population did so.

My main academic rival was Bill Prince, who became my closest school friend. We used to travel in the same direction home, frequently spending our bus fares on Bounty Bars and walking the three miles home together. We also used to spend summer evenings with several other schoolmates playing cricket. Suffice to say, I was not very good at cricket, nor any other physical activities, and my school reports, although always good, contained a headmasters caveat about getting involved in sport. Generally, I would have done if I had any ability apart from cross country running. The school was situated at the highest spot in North Manchester, and running in shorts and singlet in the middle of winter in the exposed environment obviously did not appeal.

My six form photograph aged 18.

CHAPTER 3

RAILWAY TEA BOY

During my final years at school and during my time at University, from 1959 to 1966, my family circumstances were such that it was necessary for me to work during the summer holidays. Apart from the first occasion, not unsurprisingly given my interest in railways, all subsequent jobs had a railway connection.

The first summer vacation from University, I undertook a summer undergraduate mechanical engineering apprenticeship with Associated Electrical Industries (AEI) in the Trafford Park Industrial Complex surrounding Manchester Docks. This included a time on the shop floor wiring the bogies of electrical multiple units. My workplace was underneath the glass roof of an erecting hall. It was a very hot summer, and temperatures rose to over one hundred degrees Fahrenheit. That and the early start times were an early introduction to the discomfort and tedium of shop floor labour.

Another summer, I worked on the railway parcel vans based at Manchester Victoria Station. This was an early introduction to the "Spanish Practices" that then bedevilled British commercial life. Although supposed to start work at 8 am, several of the regular workers worked a system whereby on a rota basis, one of them went in and clocked everybody else in, and they then turned in hours later! Unfortunately, I succumbed and became part of this dishonesty, but again, my exposure to such practices was useful in my future career.

However, the job I did most summers was my most educational experience, even more so than all my time at School and University. It involved providing refreshments on trains by going up and down the corridors with a trolley which comprised an urn of tea and shelves containing orange squash, finger sandwiches, crisps, cakes and biscuits. To semi-formalise the role, I was provided with a clean starched white jacket every day.

Normally, I was based at Manchester Victoria Station, and my frequent weekday task was to service two return trips to North Wales from the adjacent, now demolished, Manchester Exchange Station. The first train was a mid-morning one conveying mainly day-trippers, which I travelled on as far as Rhyl. I returned to Manchester Exchange at lunchtime. I then replenished my supplies, including tea, before working the 1630 hrs Llandudno Club Train.

Club Trains were the expresses provided mainly for businessmen who commuted from their seaside homes to their places of business in Central Manchester. As well as the Llandudno Club Train, there were others, notably from Blackpool and Southport, but Llandudno was my speciality. My rostered destination was again Rhyl, but frequently the Club Train was delayed by bridge repairs near Chester, and in order to make my booked return train and allow time to replenish my tea urn, I had to detrain at Prestatyn.

Prestatyn, unlike Rhyl, did not possess a refreshment room, so I made an arrangement with the porters whereby, for a consideration, they had sufficient boiling water ready for me in their cabin for me to replenish my tea urn. The return train mainly carried the returning day-trippers, and selling to them involved a different approach to the businessmen on the Club Train who were mainly in first class.

The North Wales run was not my only regular weekly one. I also had a roster that took me from Manchester Victoria to Barrow-in-Furness. Because of the time the journey took, this was a single out and back trip. However, the outward journey was complicated. It involved loading my reserve supplies on the Barrow train whilst taking and servicing an earlier Blackpool train as far as Preston. At Preston, I then picked up the Barrow train, praying all the time that no one had pilfered my reserve supplies. Fortunately, no one ever did. The fact that they were stored, as was normal, in a guards van generally in sight of the guard probably helped.

One bonus of both the North Wales and Barrow runs was the seascapes of the Dee Estuary and Morecambe Bay, which I was able to take in during the rare moments when I could relax. They were even rarer because, towards the end of each trip, I had to do a stock take and reconcile that with the cash I had collected. This was, naturally, before the days of credit cards etc, and cheques were, of course, a no-no. The demands of the job also meant I had to curb my interest in railways, although I generally was aware of what type of locomotive was pulling the train I was working. Almost invariably, this was a Stanier Black 5.

My weekend destinations were more varied and included Scarborough, Pontypool Road and London Euston, the latter being in the throes of its rebuilding during the electrification of the West Coast Mainline. For trains to southern destinations, I picked up my trolley and supplies from Stockport Edgeley, travelling there via Manchester Piccadilly, where incidentally I once spent a week as stand-in cellarman.

The job was at times physically demanding, particularly at weekends when instead of the normal three-gallon tea urn, a five-gallon one was employed. The loading and unloading of the trolley plus urn and boxes of extra supplies I normally had to do on my own, often in the limited time whilst a train was stopped in a station. Transferring them from the refreshment rooms to the platforms and back also was an effort. It usually involved using a platform trolley that normally carried parcels and mail, sometimes facing objections from railway and post office platform staff.

The distances involved could be significant, none more so than that from the Manchester Victoria refreshment rooms to Exchange Station, along the platform that joined the two, which was reputed to be the longest railway platform in the world. When working my North Wales roster, I had, of course, to do this four times in a day. This physical activity did not stop when I was on board a train. They could be up to twelve carriages in length, usually of varying height so that jockeying the trolley across the gangway connections between carriages involved lifting it. The trolley often having wonky wheels did not help this process.

However, the physical demands tended to pale into insignificance compared to the mental demands of the job. Apart from the scheduling of passes along the train and replenishing of the urn and trolley, there was the calculation of what to charge each customer. This was pre-decimalisation and hand calculators and was further exacerbated by the different prices of each item. Tea was sixpence a cup, orange squash seven pence whilst cheese finger rolls and ham finger rolls were ten and eleven pence respectively. The price of other items varied, but the excellent slab cake at sixpence a slice was always popular.

Apart from the educational aspect of the job, the other benefit was the money I earnt which was not insignificant. Although the basic wage was low, it was not unknown for me to work an eighty-hour week, and there was also a commission of sixpence for every pound of takings. Sometimes, I even got tips, particularly from the first-class passengers on the Club Train. However, the biggest perk was the extra to be made from the tea sales. We were given packets of tea, each of which was supposed to brew one gallon of tea. At the end of each journey, the unused packets and any unsold tea in the urn were added up and subtracted from the amount I set out with, and I had to hand in monies equivalent to the difference. This was calculated on the basis of 24 sixpenny cups per gallon.

When brewing the tea, the contents of the packages were placed inside a cage inside the urn called an infuser. The urn was then filled with boiling water and then left to brew for several minutes before the infuser and spent tea leaves were removed. One was supposed then to replace the infuser after disposing of the spent tea leaves. However, the practice was then to top up the urn with further boiling water without replacing the infuser. By these means, one could sell an extra gallon and a half of tea worth eighteen shillings per urn filling, which went straight into one's own pocket tax-free. The negative aspect was, of course, one was fuelling the generally accepted opinion of the strength of railway tea, although I tried to mitigate this by allowing the tea leaves to stew an extra time before removing them.

One incident of which I was particularly ashamed was connected with the tea urn. When changing trains at Prestatyn, after refilling my tea urn at the Porter's cabin on my arrival platform, I had to push my trolley over a crossing to the departure platform. One day whilst doing this in a hurry, my trolley's little wheels got stuck in the gap alongside the rails. The trolley tipped up, and I lost a significant amount of freshly brewed tea. This I replenished with cold water from the hydrant at the platform end normally used for watering steam locomotive tenders. Not surprisingly, the quality and temperature of the tea invoked a number of negative comments from those I served it to.

I countered these by explaining British Rail was experimenting with cold tea, which was all the rage in Belgravia and Mayfair. Possibly, due to the power of my marketing, there was only one customer who persisted with their complaint and asked for their money back. Based on this experience, in later life, I was always insistent that whatever I was involved in had a more-than-adequate marketing budget.

Another school of life lesson occurred when at the naïve age of seventeen, I was working a train back from London Euston. Whilst pushing my trolley along a corridor, I was confronted with an identical trolley coming the other way. The operative, a rather tarty youngish woman and I naturally had an altercation as to whose train it was. We compared paperwork and discovered we had both been allocated the same train, and neither of us was at fault.

Later, we chatted, and I asked her whether she was making much money. "Naw", she said, "I am thinking of going back on the game!"

Sex and trains seemed to go together. Quite often, when working late evening trains, I would find the compartment blinds drawn. Undaunted, I would open the doors and chant my mantra, "tea, squash, rolls, crisps, biscuits, etc, feigning to ignore the varying degrees of intimacy that were going on inside the compartment. Inevitably, the inmates would throw money at me for the most convenient of the contents of my trolley to get rid of me.

The basic pay of a tea boy was very low, but the combination of working an eighty-hour week and extras made my total income significant. The extras included tips, sixpence in the pound commission on sales and the money made from the tea "fiddle".

My later years saw me sampling all levels of railway catering, including Pullman and even the Orient Express. In so doing, I was never clear whether my time as a tea boy made me a more discerning or a more understanding client. Probably, it made me a little of both.

CHAPTER 4

UNIVERSITY

The family had no history of anyone going to University, but I was not aware of any thoughts that I would not go, given my academic prowess at School. It was clear that I would get a grant, given the family circumstances, which reduced the financial considerations somewhat, particularly as I was awarded a State Scholarship with a grant level marginally higher than the local authority awarded.

When it came to which Universities to apply to, the School guided me. At the time, I just accepted their suggestion for my first choice: Kings College London. However, in later years I wondered why I was not put forward for Oxbridge, given my advanced and scholarship level grades, and particularly as some of my fellow pupils with lesser grades were put forward and did go up to Oxford or Cambridge.

However, Kings London it was, and early in spring of 1962, I, along with two schoolmates who also had interviews in London that day, travelled to the capital. I remember emerging from the tube at High Holborn and walking down Kingsway to the Aldwych. My only memory of the interview itself was explaining how my interest in railways, particularly locomotives, and my construction of Meccano models were my reasons for wanting to read Mechanical Engineering. I must have been sufficiently persuasive because I was awarded a place without reservations, and hence I had no reasons to visit my reserve choices, which included Manchester and Bristol.

I went up to Kings on the second of October 1962, taking the 8.00 am train from Manchester Piccadilly. My mother and brother John saw me off. The latter later that day attended my old school speech day, which was in the famous Manchester Free Trade Hall. If it were not for the fact that I had to start at University that day, I would have been there to collect my sixth form prize. Obviously, this was a disappointment, but it was probably for the best because it took some of the pressure off my brother, who had just started at North Manchester, in terms of emulating my success, a cross he was to carry for his first few years there.

The train journey to London was rather a metaphor for my subsequent University career. The diesel locomotive hauling it broke down at Crewe and had to be replaced by a steam locomotive causing me to be three and a half hours late arriving in London. Purely by chance, on the tube, I bumped into the only old boy from North Manchester who had preceded me to Kings in recent years. He persuaded me that registration that day was not obligatory and led me to the Cheshire Cheese pub in Surrey Street, alongside Kings. This has long since been demolished and replaced with office development and is not to be confused with the famous Cheshire Cheese pub, which is in Fleet Street.

Before going up to Kings, I had reserved accommodation in a hall of residence in Champion Hill just south of Camberwell. I was in the main building, a large, old house called Platanes, which we always referred to as Plats. I arrived there in time for dinner to be reunited with my belongings. These had gone ahead in a trunk, which I had entrusted a few days before to the British Rail carrier service.

University is not supposed to equip one with an academic education but a much broader experience, particularly if one moves away from home. This was particularly true in my own case, and for the first time in my life, I had money in my pocket. Apart from rubbing shoulders with fellow students from a variety of backgrounds, which in my case, having elected to read engineering meant males, living in Platanes meant exposure to the opposite sex.

Plats was close to Kings College Hospital at Denmark Hill, and there were numerous opportunities at hops parties etc, to meet nurses and physiotherapists working or training at the Hospital. The Wednesday night hop at the Hospital Rugby Club at Dog Kennel Hill was a regular venue. Inevitably, I started going steady with a blonde nurse. To my later shame, I broke the relationship off in an abrupt and rather ungentlemanly way when I decided that I did not want to get tied down at such an early age.

At Kings itself, the Engineering Society also played a significant part in my social life. Kings had a stone lion mascot called Reggie, who was regularly hijacked by students from other colleges, so raids had to be carried out to effect his recovery. We, at Kings, similarly hijacked the mascots of other colleges, notably Queen Mary's lioness, Mary, and Northampton College's, now City University, carrot.

It was on behalf of the Engineering Society that I arranged the first of several Thames Riverboat Parties, which became one of my "things" over the years. I also wrote for and acted in several satirical cabaret shows.

I also indulged in several student pranks. One of these concerned a South London building contractor called Syd Bishop. It was his company's practice on every demolition site on which they were working to erect a substantial wooden sign with "Syd Bishop, Demolition Contractor Camberwell – Watch em come down". As fast as these signs were erected, we would take them down and store them under the snooker table at Plats. It may be apocryphal, but I was told that, scratched on the Parthenon atop the Acropolis in Athens was "Syd Bishop, Demolition Contractor Camberwell – Watch em come down".

However, these goings-on were typical of any normal student's life, but Kings provided the extra dimension of being in London, and I was there at the height of the swinging sixties. Lunchtimes were often spent across the Strand at the Lyceum Ballroom, and it was there that I heard my first Beatles Number – "*IWant to HoldYour Hand*".

One of the students at Kings was also part of a pop duo, Peter and Gordon, which had a major hit. Peter Asher also had a sister Jane who went on to be a famous actress and cake maker and girl friend of Paul McCartney. She and other pop celebs used to frequent a boys club, The Lion Club in the East End, where Kings Students used to help out, and I was on the periphery of the scene that used to frequent events there. My other involvement with the London Pop Scene of the time was as Carnival organiser, or rag, as it was known at other Universities, and this involved charity concerts with the pop notables of the day.

Meanwhile, I did not neglect my other interests and watched City whenever they played in London and also, Kings had a railway society which I joined and regularly visited locomotive depots around London. Remarkable as it might seem, I also found time to go home. This was inevitable during the vacations for financial reasons, but I also used to go home each half-term. The Euston line was being electrified at the time, so most London to Manchester trains went from St Pancras to Manchester Central with the bonus of the northern part of the journey being through the very scenic Peak District. I even fitted in visiting the family down in Wiltshire, staying with Aunt Nellie.

One particularly memorable trip from Paddington was on a very foggy November Friday night, which brought to mind the Peter Cook and Dudley Moore sketch of Sherlock Holmes and Doctor Watson taking a Paddington train in similar circumstances intoning, "pray God we get there in time".

Unfortunately, I got the balance between the wider experience and my academic studies wrong to the detriment of the latter. The writing was on the wall at the end of my first year when I had an unheard of failure in Engineering Drawing. It did not help me in that I was parsimonious and did not purchase a reasonable standard drawing kit. I rectified this in my second year and passed when the time came to re-sit but still did not mend my academic ways. Inevitably as examination time approached, I must have sensed this because I became quite ill. Although I recovered in time to take the examinations, I not unsurprisingly failed most subjects. Nevertheless, I would not offer any excuses; it was simply down to me skipping lectures and not doing enough work. The only redeeming feature was I successfully re-sat my first year of Engineering Drawing.

I was therefore sent down but with the opportunity of re-sitting in the summer term of the following year, 1965.

Stan Price

CHAPTER 5

"GAP YEAR"

To me, it was a no-brainer that I should return to University and re-sit my examinations the following summer. However, I would have to pay for it myself, as my state scholarship would not fund it. For this reason alone and also simply to support myself, it was imperative that I got a job. The short-term was covered by my usual tea boy job on the trains, but something more long-term was obviously required. At the end of my university degree course, I would have to take up a two-year graduate engineering apprenticeship, so it occurred to me that I would minimise the impact of me being sent down, at least in terms of time, if I took up a similar engineering apprenticeship until it was time to return to Kings. I therefore approached a number of engineering companies in the Manchester area to see if they would take me on.

Hawker Siddeley Aviation (HSA), based at Chadderton near Oldham, granted me an interview and subsequently offered me a technician apprenticeship post, which I accepted. The Chadderton factory was originally owned by the AVRO company, manufacturer of such aircraft as the Lancaster and Vulcan bombers. The sister factory in Woodford Cheshire I had, of course, visited as a child whilst they were manufacturing the Vulcan. And so, after my usual stint on the trains and a holiday, partly with friends in the South of France, I reported to HSA.

The first six weeks at Chadderton were spent in the Apprentice Training School, where I was taught a number of manual fitting tasks such as filing and operating machine tools such as millers. The company also insisted I enrol on a Higher National Diploma (HND) course in mechanical engineering. I presume they were safeguarding themselves in case I decided not to return to Kings or, if I did, failed again. Cynically, it occurred to me that with me, they were getting a university quality individual on a technician's pay. The HND course was an evening one at Salford Technical College. After Kings, I found the course extremely easy and, with due modesty, found myself head and shoulders academically above the other students on the course.

After the six weeks in the Apprentice Training School, I was let loose on the shop floor. Here I was employed, under supervision, riveting the aluminium skins onto the wing framework of the HSA748's, which were being manufactured at the time. The 748 and its military equivalent, the tail loading door 780, was a twin Rolls-Royce Dart engined replacement for the Dakota. The aircraft was a commercial success, with over 300 being built and sold worldwide.

This time on the shop floor, as well as being beneficial in terms of work experience, was useful in other ways. Firstly, it instilled into me the discipline of early working days – I had to clock in at 7.30 am. Secondly, it gave me further insights into the Spanish Practices which bedevilled the UK manufacturing industry at the time. A specific instance was one employee who clocked in every morning and spent the whole day until he clocked off reading the Sporting Chronicle in the toilets. Although this was well known, presumably also to management, nothing was done about it.

This guy's modus operandi was the source of one of the scripts I wrote for the Apprentice Association Christmas Pantomime with which I had got involved. The pantomime was held in a hall at the now-defunct Belle Vue Pleasure gardens and was attended by senior management who seemed not to take too much umbrage at their being lampooned within it.

To organise the pantomime, we were given an office in the middle of the shop floor. This caused some excitement amongst the surrounding workers as the office was used to audition girls from the offices for female roles in the various pantomime sketches. One day, two senior foremen, distinguished by white coats with light blue collars, poked their heads round the door of the office whilst I was sat there scriptwriting and asked why a constant stream of girls was visiting the office as it was causing so much comment. I do not know if my answer – that it was Ministry of Defence confidential – satisfied them, but I did not get a repeat visit.

I was not successful with all the girls employed at the factory. During my first week there, I attended the weekly hop at the Work's social club. Being bronzed and fit from my recent sojourn in the South of France, I confidently asked an attractive contemporary bird's nest beehive-hair styled girl to dance. I was utterly shocked when she answered, "fuck off".

My stint on the shop floor lasted until Christmas, and in the New Year, I was transferred to the Metallurgy Laboratory. This was no coincidence because the topic in which I had fared worst at Kings was metallurgy. The laboratory, amongst its run-of-the-mill metal quality control functions, was heavily involved in investigating the properties of titanium. The reason for this was that titanium was to be extensively used in the next aircraft type the factory was to produce. This was a long-range four jet-engined strategic freighter for the Royal Air Force (RAF) designated the HS681.

A device had been produced to oscillate titanium strips and to record their natural period of oscillation. The dimensions of the metal strips were measured, and using these and the period of oscillation, Young's modulus could be calculated. The device allowed the strips to be held in either a fridge or a furnace, both of which allowed them to be held at a controlled temperature so that Young's modulus could be calculated across a wide temperature range. A vast number of strips was used, and this plus the temperature range meant that hundreds if not thousands of repetitive calculations needed performing.

The potential for boredom I viewed with dismay until someone pointed out the factory had a device called a computer which would take the tedium out of the task. Furthermore, actioning this involved talking to an attractive blonde girl called Lesley. The double attraction of effort saving and romance meant inevitably that I went down this route.

This was my first brush with computers and involved writing a short program to perform the calculations in what was called a Tabular Interpretive Scheme (TIS).

TIS was effectively a spreadsheet, except rather than putting the numbers and formulae on a screen, they were written on a paper proforma in the form of a grid. The contents of this grid were then punched onto a paper tape, and this was fed into the computer, which then applied the formulae to the numbers and printed out the resultant amended grid. The computer that was used was a very early valve computer - the Ferranti Pegasus Mark 1*.

Using the computer did indeed significantly reduce my workload, but in the end, it was to no avail. The Government cancelled the HS681 Project simultaneously with the TSR2 strategic bomber and the 1154 vertical take-off supersonic fighter. Although the HS681 Project was not as far advanced as TSR2, which had flown, there was already a full-sized mock-up at Chadderton, and the cancellation was a bitter blow to the whole company.

Meanwhile, I had been moved on from the Metallurgy Laboratory to Sales Engineering. There I was principally involved in calculating the performance of the HS748 on prospective customers' routes. The calculations took into account route characteristics. These included the characteristics of the relevant arrival and departure airports – runway lengths, altitude, ambient temperatures plus the distance between the two and the required fuel reserves. The results were then put into a brochure which, in turn, became part of the sales pitch to the intended customer.

However, one assignment was concerned with establishing why we had lost out to the rival Japanese YS11 in equipping Olympic Airways of Greece. This was a particularly galling loss as Olympic had been leasing a number of 748s for some time, apparently with no problems. The reason given was that the YS11 was more economical, and specifically, it could carry more passengers. This was puzzling as the YS11 had no greater capacity, and obviously, the weight restrictions imposed by the route characteristics were the same for both aircraft types. Hawker Siddeley had got access to the calculations on which Olympic had based its decision, and I analysed these. It soon became apparent that instead of using the normal figure of 200lbs per average passenger with baggage, the YS11 sales brochure had used the Asian figure of 180lbs. Deducing this, of course, made no impact on the Olympic decision but obviously helped alert our sales team to any future unfair comparisons.

I stayed in Sales Engineering until the Easter of 1965 when it became time to return to Kings.

Stan Price

CHAPTER 6

ACADEMIC REDEMPTION

I returned to Kings at Easter 1965 to repeat the second year summer term, along with several colleagues who also had failed their second years. The fact that there were several in the same position led to one controversial incident. The fluid dynamics lecturer pontificating on wave theory stated that fluid particles accelerated into the crest of the wave. John Lloyd, a fellow returnee, put his hand up and pointed out that the lecturer the previous year had said the fluid particles decelerated into the crest of the wave. The lecturer uncharitably snapped - "not listening was why you failed".

At this point, Dave Forbes, yet another returnee, stood up and gave a detailed explanation of why the lecturer had been correct the previous year. After a pause, the lecturer reluctantly concurred. I could not restrain myself and asked what it would be on the date of the Fluid Dynamics examination. The embarrassed lecturer reacted to my sarcasm by asking me to leave the lecture hall. Fortunately for me, I heard nothing more about it.

An academically more interesting situation that repeating the course revealed was my understanding of vibration theory. The previous year, typically, I had missed the first ten minutes of the first lecture of the vibration theory course. When I arrived, the board was already covered in algebraic equations, and this continued for the rest of the lecture series. What I had missed was the diagram of the situation from which the algebraic equations were derived. This consisted of a weight hanging on a spring with an extension of the weight in the form of a piston being immersed in a viscous fluid in a cylinder. If I had attended these first ten minutes and seen this diagram, I could have derived all the algebra that followed.

Unlike the first two years, I was not in University accommodation for the term. Instead, along with Dave Forbes, I lodged with a family in Nunhead, South London, overlooking the local cemetery. This remoteness from the social life at Kings was probably a factor why I was able to get my head down and study with the result that I successfully passed all my re-sits and was therefore given the go-ahead to continue to a final, third year, of my degree. However, a more important factor in why I, at last, was diligent about my studies was the shame at having failed so dismally first time around.

To discover my fortunes in the re-sits, I had to interrupt my summer tea-boy job and travel up to London. Given the good news, I decided to celebrate on the journey back by having the full Monty dinner in the restaurant car of the crack Mancunian express that left Euston at 6.00 pm. Inevitably this involved a starter drink and a full bottle of wine, followed by brandy. This was much to the consternation of the elderly clergyman who sat opposite to me. His appearance was like a character in a Trollope novel, and I learnt later he was the Archdeacon of Manchester who rejoiced in the splendid name of Selwyn Bean.

Luckily, my having to repeat a year did not jeopardise my entitlement to the third year grant of my State Scholarship, so there were no difficulties in my taking up the chance of completing my degree. For accommodation, I shared a flat in Herne Hill, again in South London, with Dave Forbes and John Lloyd, who also had flunked their second year. The fourth flat member, Paul Kitchen, was a medical student at Kings College Hospital who later went on to be an eminent ear, nose and throat consultant.

A further two medical students occupied the flat upstairs, and downstairs were four nurses and a physiotherapist.

Not wishing to repeat my previous academic disaster, I again diligently attended to my studies and successfully passed my finals. However, because of my second-year failure, I graduated with only a pass degree. Interestingly, amongst the most successful students of my original intake were two serving RAF officers who both got firsts.

A major part of my third-year course was a design exercise, the object of which, in my case, was the bogie of a railway electrical multiple unit which, of course, given my railway interest, I had chosen. This presented a particular problem in satisfying the weight-bearing requirements, spatial and extension characteristics of the secondary suspension. The only way I could see to satisfy all the requirements was to use two springs where there would normally be one, with one spring inside the other. This meant both springs had to synchronise their extension and contraction without conflicting with each other. To choose springs with the characteristics that met these criteria meant continuous, repetitive calculations that showed no signs of converging, so for the second time, I invoked the assistance of a computer.

Fortunately, we had been given a course on computer programming using the Extended Mercury Auto code (EMA) language on the London University Atlas computer, to which Kings had a "fast link". I therefore wrote an EMA program to perform the calculations, which did eventually converge, so I was able to produce a practical design.

My becoming a diligent student did not mean I totally neglected my social life, the highlight of which was the party to celebrate the end of our final examinations. This was held in our flat in Herne Hill and went on to the wee small hours. By the end, the record player was playing only four numbers:

"*Paint it Black*" by the Rolling Stones,
"*Strangers in the Night*" by Frank Sinatra,
"*California Girls*" by the Beach Boys, and
"*River Deep - Mountain High*" by Ike and Tina Turner.

The repertoire was not to everyone's taste, or perhaps it was the volume because about 3 am we received a visit from the Constabulary. However, after an affectation of diplomatic humility, we got away with a warning, and none of us was dragged off to the local police station.

My social association with Kings and my fellow students did not end straight away, and for several years I regularly returned to London for purely social reasons. Perhaps the most memorable of these was the Commemoration Ball prior to the Christmas of my graduation year, 1966. I travelled up to London in the evening, changing into black tie and tails in the train toilet.

I was met at Euston by my partner for the evening in her Triumph Spitfire sports car. She drove it onto the roadway beside the arrival platform, so I simply stepped from my carriage into her Spitfire, much to the envy of my fellow male passengers. What I did not know, until later, was that despite the tight turning circle of the Spitfire, she had managed to put one wheel over the platform edge just as the train was arriving. It says much for her competence and charm that she inveigled several railway staff into manhandling it back onto the platform before a disaster ensued.

The following May saw the graduation ceremony in the Albert Hall with degrees being presented by the Chancellor of London University, The Queen Mother. Naturally, my Parents attended, although Auntie Nellie attempted to supplant my father. My overwhelming emotion was delight in their pride. It was, however, tempered by the zip on my trousers giving way before the ceremony and my hoping that the resultant safety pin did not show when I made my bow to the Queen Mother. The actual awards ceremony was then followed by an impressive service in Westminster Abbey.

Stan Price

CHAPTER 7

START OF A CAREER

Hawker Siddeley gave me the chance of resuming my employment with them once I had obtained my degree. It made sense to do so, one of the advantages being I had no need to go for interviews with other companies. Also, National Service had been abolished, so that was not a consideration, much to my relief. Therefore, after a couple of months of lucrative employment as a railway tea boy, followed by a continental holiday, I reported back to Chadderton.

Immediately I was told I would be continuing my employment in the computer services department at Woodford and was driven down there by the overall head of computer services, Pete Morton.

Computer Services Woodford did very little commercial computing, its prime function being to support the technical design departments, including aerodynamics, performance, weights, stress and flight test. The only non-technical system that it was involved with that I could recall was one for production control using programme evaluation and research techniques (PERT), which included critical path analysis.

Unfortunately, a typical run of the system took some thirty-six hours, and the Ferranti Pegasus Computer on which it was hosted seemed to break down daily! Nearly all the programming that was done in Computer Services Woodford was for the Pegasus and was done in either machine code or in Pegasus auto code. The Pegasus was unable to support the third-generation languages, Algol, Fortran and Cobol, that were then becoming commonplace.

Input and output to the Pegasus were via five-track paper tape. The contents of the tapes were printed out on teleprinters of which there were several in the Department. Unfortunately, when a machine code program was being printed out, the Pegasus did it in a block, followed by another block. With a block only being some eight characters wide, there was a considerable amount of unused blank paper on the right-hand side of printouts. I believe it was my idea but the first machine code program I wrote provided the facility of printing out the blocks in columns, the number of which could be specified, so saving paper.

The Pegasus was very much a first generation computer with valves and mercury delay lines requiring an air-conditioned environment. It had a 39-bit word architecture with two machine code instructions per word, plus a sign/check digit. The "fast" store comprised eight, eight-word blocks. One of these blocks constituted the accumulators. Most of the storage was an 8k-word drum. Waiting for the drum to rotate in order for a block to become available was time-consuming, and one of the arts of machine programming the Pegasus was to optimise when blocks on the drum needed to be available to reduce waiting delays.

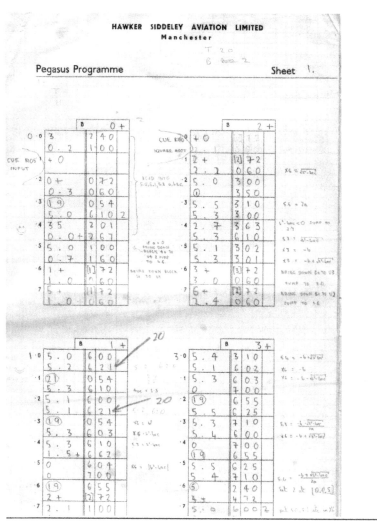

An Example of Pegasus Machine Code

Another early program, which I wrote in auto code and was typical of the work of the Department, was to simulate the performance of a revolutionary type of aircraft. This was a blown pole, which, as the name suggests, comprised a pole rotating above the aircraft from which air was blown to create effectively a wing - rather like one blade of a helicopter. At times it was difficult to discover when the program crashed whether it was a programming error or that the aircraft had indeed crashed. Each one of these design projects was given a unique number, and this one was 806. Not many of these "paper" aircraft actually saw the light of day but those that did include:

- 698 – The Vulcan.
- 707 – The Vulcan third scale prototypes of which there were three. Not to be confused with the Boeing of the same number.
- 748 – Which never got a name.
- 780 – The Andover, which was a military rear freight door version of the 748 for the RAF. Ten of which were sold on to the Royal New Zealand Air Force.
- 801 – The Nimrod.

Apart from a brief time back at Chadderton, I spent the rest of my apprenticeship in Computer Services Woodford and eventually joined the Department. Even the spell back at Chadderton was connected with computers – programming the instructions for numerical controlled machine tools. The programming resulted in tapes for the machine tools themselves produced by Ferranti at Dalkeith.

As well as programming, I operated the Pegasus during an evening shift. One of the naughty practices we got up to was to modify programs so they ran longer. For example, it was possible to reduce the increments in calculating an aircraft's take-off performance so as to make the computer spend longer performing a given run. As well as increasing the hours that were worked on the shift, hence getting paid more, it meant we could leave the computer running for a predictable length of time so we could slope off to the pub. (The Thieves Neck, a Robinson's House in Woodford Village.)

Upon my return to Manchester, I had started living in the family home in Cheetham, North Manchester, and the commute to Woodford was extremely difficult by public transport. Fortunately, several of my colleagues made a similar commute, and I was able to get lifts on the basis of petrol sharing. Sometimes, after spending an evening in London, I would get a night sleeper to Manchester Piccadilly and then the local train out to Poynton (Lower Poynton the line of my childhood to Higher Poynton having been closed) where I would arrange for someone to pick me up.

However, driving and owning a car was clearly desirable, so eventually, I purchased a Morris Mini. Even before my driving test, I used this to get to Woodford accompanied by a colleague who was a qualified driver. This was useful practice for my driving test, and this, plus my father's expert tutelage, meant I passed my driving test first time.

Eventually, I stopped being a graduate apprentice and became a full-time staff member of the Computer Services Department. Straight away, I was given the job of writing a Pegasus machine code program to analyse the fight test readings for the bomb bay heating system of the Mk 1 Nimrod.

The readings were put on paper tape, which was read by the program I wrote. Each reading was then calibrated against a table specific to the particular sensor that produced the reading. There was a magnetic tape-based library of these tables, but the routines that created, updated, etc, this library was not my responsibility. My program went on to perform a number of limited calculations, highlighting the results of these calculations where an answer might indicate there was a problem with the equipment.

One of my colleagues was given a similar assignment with respect to the cabin conditioning systems on the Nimrod. Both of us were instructed to use fixed-point rather than floating-point routines to perform the calculations. This would have involved writing the more complex code required to handle fixed-point arithmetic. However, there was a complete set of subroutines available in the Pegasus for floating-point calculations. I therefore decided to disobey my instructions and did the calculations in floating-point. This resulted in me finishing the assignment a couple of months before my colleague who stuck to the fixed-point brief. Nobody spotted what I had done, and the accuracy of my program appeared unaffected, so I gained a distinct advantage in the Department pecking order.

This advantage soon resulted in my being put on monthly staff, which meant I no longer had to clock in and could lunch in the Senior Staff Canteen. There were, in fact, six "canteens" for the different grades of staff starting with the works canteen for shop floor workers, up to the Directors Dining Room. The Senior Staff Canteen was the fourth in the hierarchy and offered the luxury of waitress service. However, along with these privileges came responsibilities. My job title changed from Programmer to Systems Analyst, which meant I now specified and designed systems and was in charge of the team responsible for implementing them.

My first major one was for the production of the Operating Data Manuals (ODMs) for the Manchester designed aircraft. The ODMs, as the name suggests, indicated to pilots how the aircraft could safely be operated and consisted largely of tables. For example, they indicated minimum runway lengths at particular take-off weights, airfield altitudes and ambient temperature. For each phase of flight, e.g. take-off, cruise, or climb, there were three programs in the process of producing the relevant part of the particular aircraft's ODM.

The first of these calculated engine performance, which was then used by the second program to calculate raw aircraft performance data. The final program in the suite sorted this raw data into the table that went into the ODM. This presented unique formatting problems in particular as the environment got more arduous – hotter and higher. The aircraft could not operate there, so there was no entry in that part of the table.

The programs were being written in Fortran, and I discovered that the format of a particular line in a table could be built up in a variable, depending on the data that was to go in it. The WRITE statement then included the name of the variable containing the format rather than the format itself. This, fortunately, solved the formatting problem.

The development of the system and its subsequent use to prepare ODMs took place on the Manchester University Atlas computer. This was only available to us overnight on a bureau basis; so it involved the team – programmers, punch girls and the responsible performance department guy, plus myself after our normal working day travelling into Manchester University from Woodford. Actually, our first port of call was a room in the University of Manchester College of Science and Technology. This room contained a variety of equipment for the punching of cards and tapes, which the punch girls used to prepare the input for the night's computer runs. The paper tapes, in this case, were 8-track as opposed to the 5-track, which the Woodford Pegasus used as input. From there, we had dinner on expenses before proceeding to the University, where we passed on the jobs for the University Atlas Operators to run. Should these prove unsuccessful and we could identify the fault, the punch girls would make the necessary corrections, and the job would be re-submitted.

The system was eventually successful and produced the ODMs for both the 748 and Nimrod but after considerable development effort. I was particularly embarrassed when asked by the Chief Aerodynamicist in a meeting how long it would take to program the climb sort program, which I was responsible for. My answer was that I could dash it off in a couple of weeks. Unfortunately, it took me an embarrassing three months.

Even after the system was up and working, I was still responsible for troubleshooting any problems with it. One of these occurred while I was watching Manchester City play West Bromwich Albion in the Charity Shield at City's ground. The Charity Shield then was played between the previous seasons league champions and cup winners on the ground of the former.

At half-time there was an announcement: "Could Mr Stan Price please report to the Manchester University Atlas Computer Centre". City were winning 3-1 and playing particularly well, so I deferred going until the match was over when City had won 6-1.

Upon arriving at the University, I was confronted with a mass of line-printer paper. A bug in a program had caused it to go into an output loop, and it had printed the same thing out for several hours at a computer hire charge of hundreds of pounds an hour. I should have felt guilty, but the development of the system had meant I worked up to sixteen hours a day for several months, so I felt I was allowed the one lack of diligence.

Incidentally, this was my first introduction to the stressful workaholic culture of the computer industry.

CHAPTER 8

MODULAR PERFORMANCE AND DATA HANDLING

Around 1968 I was promoted to Project Leader responsible for producing and maintaining programs and systems related to aircraft performance. These included old programs that ran on the Ferranti Pegasus. Amongst these were programs that calculated the performance of the engines that were installed in Woodford Aircraft, which had been written by the Department's staff in the past. Obviously, these needed re-writing in a third-generation language to run on the third generation computers that Hawker Siddeley as a whole was purchasing and the Manchester University Atlas. There was also the need for programs that calculated the performance of new marks of the engines that were coming along.

The thought had occurred to me, whilst working on the ODM system, that surely the engine manufacturers had such programs, and if we could get our hands on them, it would save a significant amount of time and money. I therefore contacted Rolls Royce at Derby and discovered, not unsurprisingly, they had such programs but also that they were written to a US Society of Automotive Engineers standard. Furthermore, the standard required that they be made available to airframe manufacturers free of charge and that they be converted to run on the airframe manufacturers computers where necessary by the engine manufacturer.

Rolls Royce was, in fact, already doing this for the US Airframe manufacturers, most notably for the RB211 for the Lockheed Tristar. We asked that they do the same for us in respect of the Spey and Dart engines for the Nimrod and 748 aircraft, respectively. This they did, and therefore, for a time, I was regularly driving between Woodford and Derby through the beautiful Peak District national park to facilitate this.

The programs were written in Fortran for IBM 360 computers, which was Rolls standard hardware. However, the computers we were about to have were ICL 1900s, and also, some of them had to run on the Atlas for the ODM system. A certain amount of conversion work was therefore required as both the ICL 1900s and the Atlas imposed subscript range checking, whereas the IBM 360s did not. Rolls had utilised this so that multiple arrays could be accessed with just one Fortran statement. Incidentally, these programs could be used stand-alone in their own right or as subroutines to the aircraft performance programs, hence providing an integrated aircraft/ engine performance simulation package.

Having addressed the provision of engine performance programs, my attention turned to the aircraft performance programs themselves. Historically, the way that these were specified and produced was for the performance engineer to specify to a programmer the equations involved in the calculation for each aircraft type for each phase of flight – cruise, climb, take-off, etc. Thinking about it, I realised that this was extremely wasteful and that all the programs were concerned with was an object in three-dimensional space moving subject to Newton's laws under certain control parameters. At the heart, therefore, was a common module, which took inputs on weight and lift vertically, and thrust and drag horizontally, and derived the motion for an increment in time. From these increments, a trajectory in the particular phase of flight could be determined. My team and I commenced work on defining this module and the surrounding ones accordingly.

The long-term goal was a hierarchy of modules within a hierarchy of integrated programs, including the engine ones referred to above, which could model an aircraft''s total flight through all its phases. Then above that, one could model multiple flights and hence a whole airline fleet's operations.

Although the work initially commenced with my team at Woodford via the overall Hawker Siddeley technical computing committee, on which I was the Manchester representative, I managed to get the other three design sites, Hatfield, Kingston, and Brough, involved. This meant the concept was used for such a variety of aircraft, including the Trident, 125 Business Jet and the vertical take-off Harrier, as well as our own Nimrod and 748, thus further vindicating the concept.

However, there was another example of unnecessary duplication. A large proportion of the data that had to be input to a program that modelled a specific aircraft's phase of flight was common to that aircraft's other phases of flight. Therefore, it made sense to reduce the amount of data that had to be input (it had, up to then, been input from paper tape or cards each time a program was run) by storing this on computer media in a way that made it accessible to many programs. This would also have the spin-off benefits of ensuring the consistency of the data, hence reducing errors.

Again the other Hawker Siddeley design sites were involved, but unfortunately, one of them, de Havillands at Hatfield, was unreceptive to the approach I advocated for how this data was to be stored. They had for some time had a more up-to-date computer, an English Electric KDF9 and considered themselves superior to the other sites. However, the method they were still using and advocated for the new

Hawker Siddeley standard system was distinctly retrograde. They believed that data items would be identified by the physical address of where they were stored on the computer.

However, this had three immediate disadvantages:

- Firstly, it meant every programme would have the address of every data item inflexibly hard-coded in it.
- Secondly, the identification of the item would be via the meaningless physical storage address.
- Thirdly, it restricted the programs so that they could only run on one computer.

The scheme we advocated was that each data item would be tagged with a meaningful name, e.g. "wingarea", and all the programmer had to know and do was to access a retrieval routine with the name, and the routine would insert the value of the data item in the programme when it was executed.

Furthermore, as well as picking up a particular value, the retrieval routine could, if necessary, access tables and formulae, etc, to determine the value. This facility would enable the same programs to perform very simple calculations for an aircraft that was in an embryonic design stage and also handle the same calculations for more advanced designs or even actual aircraft where many more parameters were involved.

This system was termed data handling, and as for modular performance, a sub-committee of the main technical computing committee managed the project. I chaired both of these and, as a result, was able, with the help of the Brough representatives, to overrule Hatfield.

Modular Performance and Data Handling were not the only innovations I introduced to Hawker Siddeley's technical computing. Generally, the calculation statements in a computer program were written based on a particular standard set of units. However, the design teams, in line with the British engineering sector in general, were about to switch from using Imperial units to the International System of Units known as SI. This would have meant that every technical program would have to be gone through line by line to modify them so that they would handle the new system of units. I therefore had it agreed that all future programs would have the calculation statements refer to a data block in which contained the constants for the particular system of units in use. Then if the system of units changed, rather than the expensive and time-consuming trawl through every line of code, all one had to do to convert the program to function with a different system of units was to change the data block.

Generally, I attempted to ensure that the principle of not hard-coding in things that could potentially change was adopted where I subsequently had influence.

No doubt others elsewhere were introducing similar innovations, but I think I could reasonably claim to be one of the pioneers. Nevertheless, I now wish I had been smarter in recognising the commercial potential of some of my ideas. Particularly, Data Handling contained many of the concepts that are used in database technology. The term database, to my knowledge, had not been coined at the time we were introducing Data Handling.

Stan Price

CHAPTER 9

RISE AND FALL

As well as being promoted to Project Leader, I was soon acting head of the Computer Department at Woodford, after the existing head was made redundant. I was therefore responsible for over twenty analysts and programmers and also the team of "punch girls". They prepared the cards and tapes that were then the principal source of input to the Pegasus computer that was still in use and the third generation ICL 1900 Computer at Chadderton.

One of my previous actions was to secure better office accommodation for the analysts and programmers. Hitherto, they had been located at one end of a large drawing office, which had noise levels not conducive to their work. The new accommodation was in what had been the AVRO Boardroom across the shop floor from the old accommodation.

Unfortunately, the only adjacent toilet facilities were gents, dedicated for very senior executives' use, which we also were allowed to use. At the time, all the analysts and programmers were male, and the "punch girls" had stayed where they were, so the lack of facilities for females did not matter so much. When it did matter was during my weekly heads of section meeting, which included the chief "punch girl" and her deputy. Attending the meeting meant they had to run the gauntlet of wolf whistles etc, as they crossed the shop floor. Obviously, they were reluctant to do this more than was necessary, so if they required toilet facilities, we instituted the practice of me seeing that the very senior executive gents were unoccupied, and then I would stand guard outside to ensure they did not suffer any male intrusion.

I was doing this one day when Sir Harry Broadhurst, Chairman of Hawker Siddeley and ex RAF Air Chief Marshall, attempted to use the gents.

"Sorry," I said, "but you can't go in there, sir".

On being asked, "Why not?" I replied – "Because I have got a couple of girls in there, sir".

He responded, "Lucky you," and beat a retreat.

Not only was I, at the age of twenty-eight, heading up a significant department but also, as mentioned earlier, representing Manchester (i.e. the old AVRO Company) on the Hawker Siddeley Technical Computing Committee, and chairing the sub-committees on modular performance and data handling. The former meant regular travelling to London, the meetings being held in Hawker Siddeley's headquarters in Duke St, off Piccadilly.

The sub-committee meeting venues rotated around the four design sites – Kingston, Hatfield and Brough, as well as Woodford. As well as travelling to these meetings by road, rail and commercial air, I was occasionally able to use the company's private aircraft, one of which was a 125 executive jet. Although one always ran the risk of being off-loaded at short notice if a more senior executive staked a claim.

These trips were also useful for my social life, particularly enabling me to see my London based ex-college friends. If one had to stay overnight at Brough, one was booked into the pilots club, along with the Stewardesses from the evening Heathrow to Hull flight operated by British Midland's Handley Page Heralds, where some jolly evenings were had by all.

It would appear that my career was well set, but then fate took a hand. Salary increases commensurate with my newfound status had enabled me to purchase a Triumph Spitfire open-top sports car which was dark blue in colour. That was possibly one of the reasons why, although I had my lights on, early one November morning in 1970, the driver of a large Westminster saloon failed to see me. I was travelling to Woodford at about 70mph southbound on the A34 when the Westminster turned right immediately in front of me. Fortunately, the collision knocked me onto an extensive grass verge without my hitting anything further, and although seat belts were not then compulsory, I had one on.

Even more fortunately, although perhaps temporarily unconscious and being taken off in an ambulance, I physically suffered only severe bruising. Naturally, I was extremely shaken up, and it took some weeks before I was able to return to work.

The accident also left me suffering from depression and panic attacks. One interesting outcome was that, although my management role had significantly reduced the amount of programming I was doing, after the accident, I found that I could not face programming anymore. At the time, I fancifully put this down to the blow to the head I had suffered, imagining it had impaired the part of the brain that performed programming.

I now recognise that my antipathy to programming had developed sometime before the accident. Arguably, I was suffering from programmer burnout, and my earlier theory was merely an excuse. The other aftermaths of the accident – compensation, the conviction of the driver of the Westminster for careless driving and the introduction of speed restrictions on the section of the A34 where the accident occurred were scant consolation.

As far as motoring was concerned, I invested in a very sturdy Rover 2000, the Spitfire having been a write-off.

The car accident was not the only thing contributing to my condition. I was no longer acting head of the Woodford Computer Department. A permanent Head had been appointed. The individual concerned had briefly been Computer Operations Manager at Chadderton after being recruited from outside for that position. He had not proved a success, and his new appointment appeared to be merely a sideways one to remove him from Chadderton, irrespective of the impact on the Woodford Department, including myself.

This, coupled with medical advice to move from Manchester and living at home with my parents, made me resolve to do just that, and I started to look elsewhere. This alone improved my mental state, as evidenced by my selling the Rover 2000 after a year and purchasing a brand-new flame bronze coloured open-top MGB.

CHAPTER 10

"SOFTWEAR" ENGINEER

The 10th August 1972 edition of the Sunday Telegraph contained a small advertisement for Software Engineers. Although the terms Software Engineering and Software Engineer had been in existence since at least 1968, when NATO had held a conference proposing that they were the answer to the high failure rate of software projects, I had not been aware of the terms until then. This was probably a result of my not following, at that time, principally academic developments in my profession. However, given my engineering background the concept of engineering software appealed to me, and this, coupled with my desire to leave Hawker Siddeley and Manchester, made me apply.

The positions were with the Civil Aviation Authority (CAA), which had just been hived off from the Board of Trade, but nevertheless, the interviews for which I was selected were held in offices of the Civil Service Commission in Northumberland Avenue in London.

The interviews were conducted by a panel of five and included an eminent professor, and were chaired by Jim Curle, who later became Director General of Telecommunications of National Air Traffic Services (NATS), of which the CAA formed the civilian component. Despite the gravitas of the panel, I was neither nervous nor overawed, probably because my interview was at 2 pm, and I had enjoyed two or three pints with old friends beforehand. Indeed, when asked what I knew about software documentation, I replied "everything," and to my surprise, there was no follow-up question, which maybe I would have struggled with.

Despite such brazenness, I was one of three candidates offered positions, and I was later to learn that, in actual fact, they were seeking twelve, but only three measured up.

I accepted the offer, and on Sunday 3rd December, I ensconced myself in a small hotel in Beulah Hill, South London. The next morning, although feeling lousy with influenza, I reported to the CAA in the Adelphi Building, lying between the Strand and the Thames between Waterloo and Hungerford Bridges. There Jim Curle introduced me to Chris Walton, the guy who was designated to oversee these strange beasties, software engineers, plus the one who had joined a week earlier. That afternoon I had to go to the personnel department in Upper Woburn Place to perform the administrative functions required of a new recruit. December the 4th was a miserable wet day, which exacerbated my influenza, and the next morning I felt too sick to leave my bed, never mind the hotel. I did, however, manage to telephone the Adelphi and spoke to someone who I assumed to be the Jim Curle I had asked for.

It was a week or so before I felt well enough to report to the Adelphi where I discovered I had not spoken to Jim Curle but a Mr Terle, who had made no effort to pass the message on. Nevertheless, this unfortunate start was soon forgotten, and I commenced work in an office with the other two newly recruited software engineers.

The CAA had created a special telecommunications engineer grade of software engineer for their new recruits, which was equivalent to the existing grade of Signals Officer. Possibly, because the CAA and its Civil Service predecessor had little experience of recruitment at a senior level and did not operate a graduate recruitment scheme, there was inevitably some resentment to us newcomers. A trade union bulletin referred to "softwear engineering for those who wished to dabble in programming".

Another example of the rejection symptoms the organisation exhibited towards software engineers and software engineering was that when I sent things to be typed to the typing pool in the Adelphi, they were often returned. This was because the head of the pool, who it was rumoured was a concentration camp survivor, refused to let her girls type alien words, which included the new and strange-to-her terminology of the computer industry.

Nevertheless, individual CAA staff members realised our worth and were asking for our input. For example, I was asked for assistance in specifying the software for an air traffic control system to handle Concorde and presumably other supersonic flights. Not surprisingly, given that only a handful of Concorde services ensued, the system never saw the light of day.

Another cancelled project, which we software engineers were more influential with, was a system for assisting controllers in knowing more exactly the sequence of aircraft landing at Heathrow. This involved calculating the timing and speed of aircraft leaving the four stacks so that the spacings when they landed on the runway were the minimum commensurate with safety, and hence its use was optimised.

A prototype of the system was being developed by the Royal Radar Research Establishment at Malvern. One of my software engineer colleagues, Dave Neumann, and I visited Malvern and viewed the system. We discovered the software was very poorly written with very little structure. Its documentation was also very limited. Dave and I therefore reported this, and the project was cancelled.

However, these were only small projects compared to the major one with which the Directorate of Data Processing was concerned and with which I was soon to be heavily involved.

CHAPTER 11

ACROSS THE POND

First 1973 Visit

Sunday, 25th March 1973 saw me changing flights at Philadelphia International Airport. I had just flown in from London Heathrow and was awaiting a De Haviland Twin Otter to take me the short distance to Atlantic City Bader Field. It was my first time in the United States, and my first impression whilst waiting outside the terminal complex was of a lot of very large automobiles driven in many cases by elderly ladies.

My American Home.

At very short notice, the Civil Aviation Authority had asked me to be seconded to the Federal Aviation Administrations (FAA's) National Aviation Facilities Experimental Centre (NAFEC) at Pomona near Atlantic City.

For a number of years, the Civil Aviation Authority had been running a project to significantly upgrade the equipment at the London Air Traffic Control Centre (LATCC), including the main computer support. The civilian part of the project, labelled Mediator, was being handled by the Marconi Company and was based upon their Myriad computers. However, after some years of cost and time overruns, it had become evident that the Myriad computers had insufficient capacity. A decision had therefore been taken to relegate the Myriad computers to just handling military en-route traffic, whilst an "off-the-shelf" system was purchased from the United States.

The United States had 20 en-route air traffic control centres which contrasted with the United Kingdom's one. (There was a second one in the UK to cover Scottish airspace, but that was not part of the project). All the twenty US centres had essentially the same types of computer hardware and used the same software package called NAS. To cope with the differing airspace structure between these centres and other different local requirements, "adaptation data" had to be added to the basic NAS for each individual centre.

Clearly, LATCC would also have to have its own adaptation data, which meant the off-the-shelf concept was dubious from the start. However, the concept was even more dubious because of differences in the way en-route traffic was handled between the US and UK, which meant that the NAS software package itself had to be modified.

The UK decision to forego the homegrown Marconi system and purchase the American System was such a momentous one with inter-governmental involvement that final approval had to be given by the then prime minister, Edward Heath. Inevitably, this political involvement meant compromises that further watered down the off-the-shelf concept. This involved the UK's not acquiring the whole US package, but only the flight plan processing element, and not even all of that as the sub-system, called CUE, that allowed individual controllers to update flight plans was not deemed necessary for the UK. This later proved erroneous and, therefore, more of that anon.

The other principal functional half of air traffic control systems then, flight data processing being the first half, was radar data processing. The decision here was that, although the NAS package the UK was receiving contained radar data processing functions, the radar interface and display sub-systems that would enable the NAS radar elements to be utilised would be sourced separately from UK industry. Perhaps a factor in this decision was that the UK was not being charged for the basic NAS software, only for the cost of the UK only modifications to it. The computers, IBM modified 360s, known as 9020s, were also understandably being charged for.

After a day to get over jet lag, I reported to NAFEC, where I found a team of some twenty or thirty CAA personnel comprising Air Traffic Control Officers and Telecommunication Engineers liaising with the FAA and IBM personnel responsible for the NAS system. The IBM team were from the company's Federal Systems Division and comprised approximately 500 personnel, principally modifying and testing the software, largely for the US centres but also for the UK. Most of the team had been previously employed on NASA's mission control system at Houston and later would go on to work on the Trident nuclear submarine programme.

The whole software production process was controlled by an elaborate paperwork system for projected and actual software changes and for the correction of errors (bugs) discovered during operation or testing. For example, each week, a book was produced detailing the status of all bugs, and this was used as the working document for a rolling meeting. During this meeting, IBM managers reported on the status of bugs in the elements of software they were responsible for. If the bug count against a particular manager started to climb significantly, it was probable he or she would not be around much longer.

I was lucky that my previous experience at Hawker Siddeley, albeit with much smaller software teams, had led me to conceive and implement some of the measures necessary for the control of software development. Therefore, my learning curve about IBM's processes was significantly reduced. Furthermore, I had the background to understand the thinking behind them and why they were necessary, without which I could well have floundered.

My personal remit from the CAA was to get to grips with the support software for the NAS system. This support software comprised a number of tools for the support of the NAS system, principal amongst which were tools for the maintenance and administration of the NAS adaptation data; the production of simulations for the NAS system and the retrospective analysis of its performance; and the building of a NAS system from its disparate software and adaptation elements. This support software had some three times the numbers of lines of code than the NAS system itself. At that time, the amount of software, both NAS itself and support, represented 5,000 man-years of effort in both programming and testing.

Even though this was my remit, I soon became aware that, although only twenty-nine, I was the senior CAA telecommunications engineer at NAFEC and therefore was at the top table in all matters concerning the UK project. Not only that, but I was the only one in the UK team who was and had been a full-time software engineer. Interestingly, several of the air traffic control officers in the UK NAFEC team had significantly more software experience than their telecommunications colleagues, apart from myself.

This position on the top table and my experience soon led me to the conclusion that the UK was neglecting a vital matter if the NAS system was to be successfully used in the UK. This was that little thought had been given to how the UK version of the NAS software, including support software, was to be developed and maintained once it significantly diverged from the parent US version. This included the situation where someone had agreed that the UK would not require the source code for NAS and its support software: the software in the semi-intelligible form that the programmers had written, as opposed to the almost unintelligible "object" form it was in, once it had been compiled. Without this, the UK would have been incapable of developing and maintaining the software itself.

The only alternative would then have been the prohibitively expensive option of the UK paying IBM to do it. I therefore exceeded my remit by using the position to get this decision reversed. Surprisingly, the FAA and IBM appeared to have no problems with this and just added the source code to the list of what was to be supplied to the UK.

However, the UK`s acquiring the source code would have been futile without a staffed organisation to undertake the maintenance and development of the software. I made a crude estimate that the UK might require some 50 to 60 personnel to undertake this, whilst noting that, compared with the US situation, the area each of these personnel would have to cover would make their task very onerous. This I documented in a report to my superiors dated the 16th May 1973, and later in another report, I did a much more detailed estimate based on the number of lines of software code in each area of the operational software, and in each of the support packages.

This first report also highlighted other problems. Some of the support software ran on an old specialist operating system called NOSS, whilst the rest ran on a variant of the OS operating system that was used on IBM's 360 range of commercial computers. As I have said previously, the 9020 computers were basically 360s, but with some albeit key modifications.

Having the support software split between two operating systems in itself created problems, e.g. in additional staff familiarisation, but that was not all. Both NOSS and the variant of OS –OS/PCP were not multi-tasking. i.e. only one program could run on the computer at a time. This was highly inefficient in terms of the usage of a computer with the power of a 360 or 9020. At that time, 360 computers mainly ran a variant of OS labelled OS/MVT, which was multi-tasking, i.e. allowed the computer to run several programs at once. This did not matter too much to the FAA at NAFEC, where there was at least the equivalent of twenty 9020s for the use of the support and development teams. Indeed it was a common practice for NAFEC and IBM staff to book one of these 360 equivalents for their own, dedicated, hands-on use.

However, the UK was only purchasing one single processor 9020 in addition to the triple processor 9020 for the operational air traffic system, and this single processor would not have been able to cope with the amount of work required if only single-tasking was possible.

Therefore, my report recommended that the UK move to full OS operation as soon as possible with the assumption that this would be OS/MVT. This had the further advantage that OS 360 expertise was readily commercially available in the UK. Fortunately, the FAA was in the process of converting all the support software to run under OS, albeit at a slower rate than was required to meet the UK's needs. Also fortunately, NAFEC was about to set up an OS/MVT job shop similar to that which would be required in the UK.

OS/MVT operation also required further disc capacity than was currently specified for the simplex, and my Report also recommended that this deficiency was rectified. The final principal recommendation in my Report was that the UK adopts the management procedures used by the FAA/IBM.

Whatever the reaction to my Report in the UK, the FAA and IBM personnel at NAFEC agreed and supported my conclusions even though they meant the setting up of a NAS software support capability in the UK, which was to the financial detriment of IBM and indeed the USA generally. This was consistent with the open and friendly attitude of all but a very small few of the FAA and IBM personnel at NAFEC. Unfortunately, this contrasted with the little Englander attitude of a number of the UK team in the USA who often had a sneering attitude to anything American.

After nearly three months at NAFEC, I was recalled to the UK to attend a course on the 9020 and NAS that was to be given in London by the training element of IBM's Federal Systems Division. However, before leaving, I asked one of the computer savvy air traffic control officers in the UK's NAFEC team to "look after" the support software brief whilst I was back in the UK. Little did I realise the furore this would provoke.

Unbeknown to me, the air traffic and telecommunications arms of the CAA were constantly involved in turf wars as to who was responsible for what, and my action was viewed as conceding ground to the enemy by my telecommunications management in the UK.

The Summer Course in the UK

The course, which lasted for two months, was held in the Congregational Memorial Hall in Blackfriars London. It was attended by CAA air traffic controllers and telecommunications engineers and six employees of Plessey Radar Ltd. Although not yet aware of the magnitude of the task, CAA management was in the process of arranging a contract with Plessey for the support of the NAS software.

During the course, the Alligator club was formed in a local wine bar for those who were involved in the UK NAS Project. The title came from the expression "when you are up to your arse in alligators, you forget the original objective was to empty the swamp", which rather summed up where we were with respect to the project.

Second 1973 Visit

During my summer in the UK, two of my superiors had visited the FAA, and one of their tasks was to discover whether I had "upset "the Americans". Someone, whether miffed at my overturning some of the decisions they had taken about source code, etc, or not appreciating my style, had made the allegation behind my back. However, my FAA contacts soon disabused them of the notion. Therefore, soon after the end of the course, I returned to NAFEC.

My telecommunications management need not have worried about losing control of the support software. The air traffic control officer who had looked after it whilst I was back in the UK was more than willing to have me take back responsibility for it. However, in my May report, I had also recommended that two further UK software engineers join me at NAFEC to familiarise themselves with the support software to a depth which I could not do alone, when the activity on the support software for the UK was at its highest. I was, therefore, later joined at NAFEC by two of the Plessey personnel who had been with me on the course in the UK. My understanding was that they would report to me, and whilst one of them was happy to do so, the other, who was the assistant manager of the Plessey team, pursued an alternative agenda that was clearly aimed at maximising Plessey's involvement in the project.

This clearly was not helpful to me and, more importantly, was not conducive to maintaining the essential good relations with the FAA and IBM. The latter was particularly incensed at a rival commercial enterprise having access to their intellectual property for free, and at one stage, they contemplated asking the CAA to withdraw the assistant manager from NAFEC.

Another of the recommendations in my May report was a visit "to a US site (I should have said en-route centre) to study the use of support software there". My management agreed with this, so I spent a week in the autumn of that year at Indianapolis en-route air traffic control centre. This visit, as well as accomplishing the goal of my seeing how a US centre used the support software, also had an additional outcome. A high proportion of the traffic through the mid-west airspace controlled by the Indianapolis centre was through traffic requiring few changes to its flight plans.

Furthermore, the week of my visit, the weather was consistently fine; therefore, alterations to the air traffic schedule and its flight plans were minimal. Given both these reasons, it would be expected that the use of the Centre's flight plan update system, CUE, by the controllers would itself be minimal. However, my observations were that despite these two conditions, there was significant usage of CUE by the controllers. This contradicted an earlier report by a team of two air traffic and one operations officers that generally, the usage of CUE by US En-route controllers was minimal, thus justifying the UK's decision not to purchase it.

I therefore sent a copy of the log of the Indianapolis NAS system, which showed this significant usage, back to the UK. Nevertheless, still neither CUE nor any sub-system to perform flight plan updating by the controllers was contemplated for the London Centre. This was later to cause significant problems when the NAS system went operational in the UK.

The Indianapolis visit apart, most of this, my second 1973 stint at NAFEC was spent monitoring progress on the development of the UK system software. It culminated in early December, in the lead air traffic control officer on the UK team and I agreeing with the FAA and IBM, the composition and format of the delivery of the NAS and Support Software and their documentation to the UK.

With this, my main task at NAFEC was completed, and I was able to return to the UK in time for Christmas. The tapes containing the software and its documentation meanwhile travelled by airfreight to the UK.

However, before returning, I produced a second report. This estimated the size of the organisation required to support and develop the UK system, but unlike my previous report, it was based on the actual number of lines of code in each element of the NAS and support software and was therefore much more accurate than the figures in my May report.

To do this, I had to make guestimates as to how much software a programmer could reasonably handle. The figures I used varied depending on whether:

- It was the real time NAS or batch support software.
- If support software, its criticality to the operational NAS system.

The code was in the high-level language JOVIAL (**J**ules **O**wn **V**ersion of the **I**nternational **A**lgorithmic **L**anguage) or the less comprehensible, less programmer-friendly BAL (**B**asic **A**ssembly **L**anguage).

Fortunately, the total number of staff this came to was in the same ballpark as the crude estimate in my original report, but I confess to a little nervousness as to whether I had given each individual programmer too onerous a task.

My trip home was not without its excitement. The UK was in the throes of the three-day week caused by the first miners' strike, and seats on aircraft to and within the UK were at a premium. I was indebted to my FAA opposite number, Al Cioffi, who drove me to Philadelphia from whence I caught an internal US flight to John F Kennedy (JFK) Airport, New York.

From there, I picked up a British Airways 747 Miami to Heathrow fight, which was diverted via JFK in order to get as many people back to the UK as possible. My problems were not over when I reached Heathrow, as my eventual destination was home in Manchester and there was a dearth of trains, no hire cars and only one flight. Fortunately, the CAA connection secured me a seat on this flight, and I arrived at Manchester to find my father waiting at the bar at the end of the pier with two pints of proper English beer.

Outside Work

Arriving home for Christmas was especially pleasurable. Not until some years later did my parents have a home telephone, so the only means of contacting my immediate family, when I was in the USA, was to telephone them on Saturday evenings. This was when my parents drank in the bar of the ICI Recreation Ground at the rear of the family's Manchester home, which had a public telephone. The outstanding memory of these conversations was how Lancashire my mother's voice sounded from three thousand miles away.

The first trip to the USA had happened at very short notice and had two immediate consequences. The first was that I had started to organise a riverboat party, similar to the ones I had organised as a student, on the Thames for late May, and my departure meant I had to leave the detail organisations in the hands of my brother, John. The second was that I was separated from my then-girlfriend, with whom I was, to say the least, smitten.

Unfortunately, during my first spell in the USA, I received a letter from her breaking off our relationship. At the time, I found this devastating, but it did mean I threw myself into my work even more than I had done in the past. Her departure from the scene also meant I was then able to date several American girls, and apart from the obvious pleasures, this extended my general education somewhat. For example, I now realise that one of them was what one would now call a neo-conservative with an insular view of America, which was quite staggering for one who was otherwise very intelligent.

My time in the States also enabled me to travel including a weekend break in Puerto Rico. Other weekends were spent chilling out with my father's cousin's family in upstate New York, around Rochester, and Niagara Falls.

The latter was the scene of an unfortunate incident when returning from a late-night discothèque on the Canadian side. I was in an old white Buick, accompanied by two younger female members of the family. This, and my sixties hippy attire, chains and all, lead the US immigration official on the Rainbow Bridge to disbelieve my claims that I was a British Government Official on secondment.

Atlantic City was also not without its social life, whether drinking in the Rascal House bar close to NAFEC or more sedate events with the rest of the UK team, organised by Nic and Emily Placentra, the proprietors of the Oceanaire Motel on the Boardwalk, which was where the majority of the UK team stayed. I felt it necessary to reciprocate the hospitality the UK team enjoyed, so in late November, I organised a party for our hosts at a Polish diner close to Atlantic City.

THE TRANSFER of ownership of the "software" computer programmes from the FAA to the CAA was marked at an informal ceremony at LATCC West Drayton on Tuesday July 23 1974.

The transfer came at the conclusion of the first phase of testing in which the software was shown to operate satisfac-torily in the LATCC computer system. The second phase, in which operational staff will exercise the complete system, including hardware, software, input and output equipment and operating procedures commenced on time on July 15.

On completion of this phase in November 1974, the system will be made available for final ope-rational trials at LATCC using live traffic.

Our picture shows: (l to r) Eric Wade, DP TM (A), David Thomson DP TM (S), Gordon Hurst FAA Test Co-ordinator, Harry Cherry, DD DP (A), Joe Leporati, IBM site team manager, Alan Dixon, CAA Test Co-ordinator, and Stan Price, DP software engineer.

Stan Price

CHAPTER 12

WHISTLEBLOWER

New Year, 1974, saw me based once again in the CAA's offices in the Adelphi in Central London. My principal preoccupation was chasing up the activities necessary to ensure that the NAS and support software could be adequately supported in the UK without assistance from the USA. The most pressing of these was the recruitment of a team to do this.

By April, despite my constantly pressing my superiors, there was no sign of this happening. I therefore invoked the assistance of one of my ex Hawker-Siddeley colleagues, Andy Hofton, who was then the technical editor of Flight Magazine. He arranged for an article I wrote to appear in the 18th April edition. This hypothesised that it was obvious and inevitable that the CAA would be setting up such an organisation.

Obviously, writing such an article without approval was contrary to my terms of employment and possibly contrary to the Official Secrets Act, so it was published anonymously. I wrestled with my conscience but felt it was necessary to do something to overcome what I perceived as dithering, and, in any case, I was not revealing what was happening, only postulating what could be happening.

Whether this article had any impact, I am not able to say, but eventually, the powers that be moved and an organisation approximately the size and structure that I had suggested in my two

1973 reports was set up in the autumn of that year at the London Air Traffic Control Centre (LATCC) at RAF West Drayton, just north of Heathrow Airport. The organisation became known as SADO (Support and Development Organisation).

The delay was not critical because NATS had set up a team composed of LATCC controllers and engineers equivalent to the teams that looked after the NAS system locally at each of the 21 US en-route centres. This team was able to handle the system going operational with support from NAFEC in the US, and also some FAA and IBM staff seconded to West Drayton.

Meanwhile, the NAS and support software were formally handed over in a ceremony at West Drayton on the 23rd of July, with myself being one of the official five CAA recipients. The other four were all ex-controllers.

Initially, the staffing of SADO was a problem. The CAA did not have staff with the necessary expertise, so SADO commenced work with a number of Plessey staff and Royal Air Force (RAF) personnel. Plessey had wanted the organisation to be an exclusive Plessey operation, manned and managed by them.

However, the CAA was determined that it should be an integrated organisation with CAA managers. Furthermore, the US, and particularly IBM, would not have been happy passing control of the intellectual property within the software to a UK private sector company.

Additional to the CAA, RAF and Plessey personnel within SADO was a sprinkling of IBM personnel, seconded from the USA, whose role was to ensure the smooth and effective handover of the UK version of the software and bring the UK staff up to speed.

My participation in such an arrangement was perhaps somewhat hypocritical given my preference, all other things being equal, for as much as possible in an economy being conducted by the private sector. However, I took the arrogant viewpoint that in this case, it was best that whichever sector had the best manager should be responsible and, in the case of SADO(S), that was me.

The Head of SADO was Chris Walton, and I was made head of SADO(S) with the bracketed S standing for support. SADO(S) had two arms: one arm comprised the support team for the NAS support software, and the other arm, the staff responsible for scheduling and operating the simplex 9020 computer configuration, which by then had been delivered from the US to West Drayton.

This was not without an alarm. Having safely arrived at the cargo area of Heathrow, whilst being transported the short distance to West Drayton, the lorry carrying it mounted the grass pavement on one of the intervening roundabouts. The computer slipped, damaging the front panel, and a replacement had to be shipped from the US at short notice.

The support software side of SADO(S) comprised five Plessey employees and two of the IBM team, plus one controller. The insertion of a controller was my idea because my experience indicated that it was extremely beneficial to the effectiveness of programmers if they had immediate, local access to someone well versed in the application they were programming. Although I have never questioned the wisdom of this, it did create some problems. The controller involved did not have a heavy workload, whereas the programmers were intensively worked given the volume of software they were responsible for.

The situation was exacerbated by the pay differential of the Controller receiving twice the salary of the programmers. The only solution I had to the problem was to explain the reasoning behind the situation and to stop any resultant friction from becoming personal. One of the five Plessey employees was effectively a systems programmer supporting the bureau/job shop operation. Each of the other four was dedicated to one of the four major support software packages, with the other less significant support programs spread between them.

The Simplex side of SADO(S) consisted of a data controller and a chief operator, and originally, these two were also Plessey employees. Initially, the operators were provided by an agency. The agency contract was awarded after a competitive tender exercise during which one of the agency principals offered me the use of his very attractive secretary and E-Type Jaguar for the weekend. I would be lying if I said that the idea did not appeal to me, but perhaps, fortunately, ethics prevailed, and I awarded the contract elsewhere.

SADO was therefore staffed from several sources with several different allegiances, and it required some positive actions to ensure it worked as an integrated social unit. One of these actions was to create a social arm, and fortunately, one of the Plessey guys was also principal of a sailing school situated on one of the flooded gravel pits to the west of Heathrow.

And so, once a week, the majority of SADO took themselves off there to unwind on the dinghies that were available for hire before retiring to a local pub afterwards. I also arranged a weekend away in the Lake District, travelling in a couple of mini-buses. It was based in guest houses I knew at Glenridding on Ullswater, and the whole weekend was spent walking, dining and drinking with deliberately no mention of work.

Parallel with the staffing of SADO, the bureau/job shop based on OS/MVT running on the Simplex was set up. The Simplex, as originally purchased from the US, had an insufficient number of disc drives to operate OS/MVT. Fortunately, the FAA had commissioned IBM to produce an integrated process for building NAS. Prior to this, the build process involved using a series of NOSS and OS programs which could take up to 15 hours and was prone to error. The new process required the extra disc drives that also enabled the Simplex to run OS/MVT, and it was on this basis that a successful case was made for their purchase. OS/MVT was then installed on the extra disc enhanced Simplex along with the new system build process.

By this time, three of the main support packages had been converted to OS/MVT by IBM under contract to the FAA; however, one remained. This was not originally an integrated package but, like the system build process, was a number of disparate NOSS-based programs which analysed, verified and validated adaptation data. The FAA had no immediate plans to convert these to OS, but given the criticality of maximising throughput on the Simplex, I managed to persuade my management to spend some $100,000 getting IBM to produce an integrated package running under OS. Once this was operational, it left only a few minor items of support software running under NOSS, and the SADO(S) programmers assisted by work experience students from Brunel University converted these to OS on an opportunity basis.

These conversions, along with the $100,000 one, were provided to the FAA, and I personally felt that as well as achieving my long term objective of getting rid of the NOSS OS/PCP bottleneck on the Simplex, we had provided some reciprocity to the FAA for all their assistance.

SADO(S)'s responsibility for the Simplex did not only extend to providing a bureau/job shop on it. It was also required for testing new versions of the NAS system and acting as a testbed for the development of a homegrown radar display sub-system, activities that were outside SADO's remit. Therefore, there was obviously significant pressure for access to it.

Based on my previous experience, I felt it was important that the SADO programmers and testers had the opportunity to have at least two turnarounds of their work through the bureau/job shop each working day. I therefore devised a schedule whereby the Simplex ran OS/MVT as a bureau overnight and over an extended lunchtime. The rest of the time, access was scheduled on a weekly basis by the data controller following requests for those requiring time submitted during the previous week.

Assuming that it would not be possible to happily satisfy all demands, I added an appeals procedure in the form of a bargaining meeting based on the published schedule. This was held late on the Friday before the week concerned, and I chaired it. Not surprisingly, within weeks of the commencement of this protocol, the appeals procedure had to be invoked. It was getting well past 5 pm, and the meeting was not achieving a consensus, so I announced I was prepared to carry on as long as was necessary to achieve one. Gradually, those unhappy with the schedule the data controller had produced left the meeting until only the data controller and I were left with an unchanged schedule. Luckily, this was in time for me still to catch the last train to Manchester. Also, it proved unnecessary to ever convene the meeting again.

By this time, I had settled in a flat in Ealing and commuted from there to RAF West Drayton, where the London Air Traffic Control Centre was based. RAF West Drayton was guarded by the Ministry of Defence Police. They amused me by addressing me as Mr Price when I entered and left during the week dressed in a business suit. However, at weekends when I visited casually dressed to oversee operations in the bureau, they addressed me as Stan!

During the course of the next three years, I made several return trips to the USA to liaise with the FAA on such matters as the conversion of Support Software from NOSS to OS. Perhaps with a certain amount of guilt, I did not exactly underplay the necessity for such trips.

On one of these, my return route involved flying into Newark then transferring to Kennedy Airport for my flight back to the UK. The flight into Newark was considerably late, so in order to make my flight from Newark, I took the New York Airways helicopter across Manhattan. Upon reclaiming the cost, I received an admonishment on CAA letterhead with the astonishing statement – "we do not encourage air travel".

Another return trip was on the eve of a bank holiday in the UK. This was significant because my choice of flights back to the UK included direct regular flights back to either London Heathrow or Manchester. The former meant to a lonely empty flat whilst the latter meant home and Mother's cooking. A further choice was Concorde to Heathrow for a significant price increase, although at a lower rate than the one British Airways introduced when they realised the premium fare that Concorde could command. I would, of course, have paid for the Concorde extra myself, but this was not the reason I opted for Mother's cooking. A decision which in subsequent years I have regretted when Concorde is mentioned.

Stan Price

CHAPTER 13

FRUSTRATION

After the period of intensive activity involved in the setting up of SADO, by 1975, my work had settled down to a relatively un-demanding line management function. The only significant changes were involved with staff issues. The IBM support team was gradually withdrawn from SADO generally, including the two IBM employees supporting SADO(S). The UK was therefore on its own in terms of supporting the UK version of the NAS software. It was with some gratification that the size and structure of SADO, as advocated in my 1973 report, although stretched, handled the task competently.

The five Plessey Programmers in SADO(S) switched employment and became CAA personnel. The Plessey-employed chief operator and data controller were replaced by CAA staff, both of whom had been with the organisation some time, with the former title changed to bureau manager. Likewise, the bureau contract operators were replaced by CAA personnel. All these changes were conducted in a phased way, including a necessary handover period.

Prior to the replacement of the agency operators by CAA staff, there was one amusing episode. Something went awry with the contract for agency operators, and I was summoned back from leave sailing on Lake Windermere in the English Lake District. Unfortunately, my car was at Ambleside on the east side of the lake, and I was on the west side, with only a hired sailing dinghy as my means of transport. My claim for the relevant share of the dinghy hire caused consternation in the CAA accounts department, as there was no provision for it in the staff regulations.

The work of SADO generally consisted of bug fixing and enhancements to the NAS and Support software. Some of these enhancements were significant and were particularly connected with making NAS and its 9020 hardware an integrated Flight Data and Radar Data Processing System. As noted in Chapter 11, the original flight data processing system that went operational at West Drayton was not even the complete one operational at US centres. They had the CUE sub-system, which allowed individual controller sectors to update flight plans themselves.

Instead, the system went live at West Drayton, requiring sector controllers to telephone flight plan requests to a central cell. As my observations at the Indianapolis centre in 1974 had indicated, this traffic was far heavier than NATS had envisaged. On top of that, the folly of introducing an unnecessary manual link in what was otherwise an automated system created a bottleneck that diminished the London Centre's air traffic capacity.

An interim solution was implemented by installing touch-wire devices for updating flight plans on the six busiest sector suites. These were driven by the Myriad computers that had been retained for military use after they had proved incapable of meeting their original purpose as the main air traffic computers (see Chapter 11). They then, in turn, interfaced with NAS running on the operational triplex 9020. Although this provided a solution, it introduced a complexity that impacted on the overall system reliability. It also incurred extra costs in terms of time and staff time until a proper system was engineered some years later.

However, the 9020 at West Drayton performing only flight data processing did not offer significantly more functionality than the previous computer system that had been operational there. To justify the large expenditure and effort that had gone into the procurement of NAS and the 9020, and to achieve the integrated fight AND radar data processing capability offered by the US 9020s and comparable systems around the globe, significant further work had to be undertaken. This was in three main areas.

Although the NAS software obtained from the US had within it the capability of radar data processing as well as flight data processing, this had, perhaps mistakenly, been functionally tied off at an early stage in the modification of NAS for UK use. There was, therefore, a requirement to untie it and bring its functionality up to the level relevant to the UK and to the level the US system had achieved since tie-off. Also, to modify it to interface with UK radars and whatever UK-only radar display sub-system was forthcoming. Then, develop the principally hardware interface between the 9020 and the radar heads, and produce a radar display sub-system.

An organisational issue, which was to hamper this task, was that strategic development of the NAS software (as opposed to the day-to-day operation, which was the responsibility of the West Drayton station organisation) was the responsibility of SADO, which was part of the Directorate of Data Processing. Either side of this, in functional terms, the radars and the radar display sub-systems, were the responsibility of the Radar Directorate. This sandwich arrangement naturally increased the risk of coordination errors, of which there were several.

My SADO(S) programmers had some work ensuring the NAS support software was compatible with the radar data processing changes to NAS, and there was an impact on the 9020 Simplex. This is because, wisely, before a full radar display sub-system was developed, it was prototyped with a connection to the Simplex for testing purposes. This prototype was PRDES, which stood for

Plessey Radar Display Evaluation System – Plessey being the chosen supplier. Despite the extra load on the Simplex that this produced, the scheduling arrangements I had put in place appeared to work well, although the Simplex was now in use round the clock, seven days a week.

Apart from my management role in supervising SADO(S) staff activities connected with the above, including calling in at West Drayton at weekends to check on the Simplex operators, I personally had no significant involvement. My mind therefore turned to two strategic issues.

Although only a tenth of the size of the FAA team that strategically supported the US en-route centres systems, SADO looked after only one centre, whereas the FAA team looked after their twenty en-route centres.

SADO was therefore relatively uneconomic although essential, and I postulated in an unsolicited report that it might make sense if, in the long term, more European en-route centres might be encouraged to have systems identical to West Drayton, and the cost of SADO might therefore be spread over these centres. Given European national politics, this was a rather naïve idea, although a common system between West Drayton and the Scottish en-route centre at Prestwick did not seem to me an impossible ambition.

Incidentally, post détente between the West and Russia, the latter was also contemplating using the 9020 and NAS. A Russian delegation therefore visited the UK to seek a non-US opinion of the merits of the system. The delegation included a female air force general that, despite looking like Rosa Klebb of the Bond Movie – From Russia with Love, sparked some carnal interest on the basis of the scope for future anecdotes it might provide.

NATS operated a plethora of computer system types using a variety of software languages. The cost in terms of spares holdings, staff training, etc, was immense, and again I stuck my oar in by writing a comprehensive suggestion on how the situation might be rationalised.

It was frustrating that neither of these seemed to grab the attention of senior management. Furthermore, I was advised by a member of senior management that if I kept my head down, it was probable that I would end up at that level. However, I came to the moralistic conclusion that it was unethical to put one's self-interest before doing the "right" thing, particularly in an organisation whose prime raison d'être was safety.

Inevitably, therefore, my thoughts turned to pastures new, given I was no longer achieving anything significantly useful in my present position…

Firstly I contemplated promotion and indeed was selected for a promotions board. However, I was unsuccessful, although the feedback was that I had performed much better than the management thought I would. My own assessment was that the questions asked were perhaps inevitably the dated ones of a hardware maintenance organisation, and not the wider, particularly software and more relevant to the future skill set I possessed.

My next move was to apply for a job at the next senior level but in a different arm of CAA/NATS. This was the position with the Pythonesque title "Heads of Noise", which appealed to me. The role was to lead the unit, which measured aircraft noise throughout the UK to ensure it met legal requirements. However, again I was unsuccessful, probably because those interviewing me recognised my whimsical interest in the post.

Naturally, I considered leaving the CAA, and so I applied for a number of jobs outside, without success. One was for the project manager of a very large UK defence project where the interview with the prime contractor gave the distinct impression that they expected the project to be cancelled, and the actual task was to secure as much income from the customer, the Ministry of Defence before this happened. Indeed some months after the interview, it was indeed cancelled.

One factor fuelling my desire for promotion was that three of my SADO(S) staff were the same grade as myself. However, the situation soon resolved itself. Given my roles in pointing out the need for such an organisation as SADO and planning and implementing it, I considered that I had a reasonable prospect of being next-in-line to head it. However, on a train returning to London from a visit to the Air Traffic Evaluation Unit at Hurn near Bournemouth accompanied by my boss, the Head of SADO, Chris Walton, he told me in confidence he was about to be promoted. My immediate reaction was to indicate my expectation that I would take over from him, but he told me I would be disappointed.

The appointment of the new head of SADO occurred just before my annual confidential review; therefore, this meant it had to be conducted by my line Director – that of Data Processing. He was very complimentary about the performance of SADO(S) and myself. However, at the end, he said there was one problem; namely, I got up senior management's nose. He therefore recommended I go on a 'Working with People' course. I cheekily pointed out that if my relationship with senior management was the apparent problem, why was he recommending a 'Working with People' course? To his credit, he replied, "See what I mean?"

My relationship with the new Head of SADO was interesting in that for some time, he was largely deferential to me, which hardly in one sense increased my acceptance of the situation. However, in November 1977, he suddenly announced, without consulting me, that I was to lose one of my SADO(S) programmers. This was without any mention of a decrease in SADO(S)'s workload and commitments. He also provided no analysis showing how the reduced team would cope and appeared unaware of the analytic work I had done calculating the SADO generally and, in particular, SADO(S) manning levels. I naturally fought the proposal, but this was the final straw for me, and I redoubled my efforts to find another job.

This took over a year to achieve, which allowed me time to organise a smooth handover to the successor I had chosen: the senior of my SADO(S) programmers. This handover included his accompanying me on my last liaison trip to the USA, so the vital personal contacts I had developed were maintained.

Having obtained and accepted a new position, I held my farewell at a pub in Hayes, the Garth, which had been my temporary home for some time in 1974. The attendance and the compliments that came my way were very gratifying and particularly were the cards from the USA signed by staff at NAFEC with whom I had worked. I caused some amusement in my thank-you speech by pointing out that NATS was Stan backwards and that perhaps illustrated the nature of the relationship. I also jokingly pointed out how difficult it was to take seriously an organisation that included two directors named Cox and Dicks.

Although not regretting my decision to leave NATS, and albeit being somewhat inebriated, it was with great sadness I took my leave.

Stan Price

CHAPTER 14

PRICE OF THE YARD

My new position was Systems Manager within the Engineering Department of the Metropolitan Police, aka Scotland Yard. The Metropolitan Police (The Met), the UK's largest force in every respect, was embarking on a project to implement a command and control system. This would have the purpose of real time allocation of police assets to incidents requiring their attention on a geographic basis. My role would be a key one in choosing the contractor to implement the system and then oversee its installation.

The first morning I reported to the civilian staff personnel department (now known as human resources) offices in Horseferry Road in South West London. I was immediately ushered into an induction course, which appeared to consist of very young men and women. After some time, the class was interrupted by someone asking for me. Upon making myself known, I was released from the class with profuse apologies. The class was intended for junior clerical staff, and I had been placed on it by mistake.

And so, after completing the usual new employee paperwork, I was directed to where the Command and Control project team was located. This was not in New Scotland Yard itself but in one of several nondescript office blocks situated on the south bank of the Thames close to Vauxhall. The block backed onto the main railway line out of Waterloo whilst the front had an uninterrupted view of the Thames. Fortunately, my personal office was on that side, and I had the prestigious view of the Houses of Parliament and Big Ben. Surprisingly, the office next door to mine was burgled the day after I arrived, but despite being the new boy, I was not considered a suspect.

The project team was equally divided between police officers and civilian staff like myself. It was headed by an assistant chief engineer, who had chaired the panel which had selected me and to whom I directly reported. Several of the police officers in the team had the interesting task of producing a database for the system of every street name and location in Greater London. They had a dedicated stand-alone system on which they accumulated and crosschecked the street data. This data they not only accumulated from document sources but by touring the streets themselves where necessary. This was, of course, before the days when such data already existed in digital form.

The Metropolitan Police Command and Control project team.

Naturally, the first few weeks in my new post were spent familiarising myself with the Metropolitan Police and its personnel, as well as the project itself. It soon became apparent to me that there was a major problem. Sensibly, the Met was running a pilot project in one of the Police Divisions – Y Division – that included Tottenham and the surrounding boroughs. Sensible as this was, the pilot system was so unreliable that computerisation was becoming a dirty word throughout the Met.

Obviously, a hostile user community did not bode well for the success of the main system when it was eventually introduced, so I decided to get involved with the pilot system, although strictly it was outside my remit. Presumably, whoever's responsibility it was, was quite happy for me to get on with it, and so I did. The main cause of the unreliability was that the functionality of the system was constantly being changed. I therefore decreed that no functionality changes would be contemplated until the system was stable and therefore reliable. Once this was achieved, I allowed changes but only in a controlled manner without compromising reliability.

Another potential threat to the main Project was the involvement of personnel from the Central Computer and Telecommunications Agency (CCTA) – the Government Agency responsible for all Civil Service Information Technology. They were effectively interfering with the Project by suggesting unproven theoretical ideas for both the system and how it was to be implemented. Fortunately, with the support of my boss, the assistant chief engineer, I was able to get them out of the loop.

These issues apart, procurement of the main system was being sensibly handled even before I arrived, and apart from one or two details, I did not need to attempt to change anything. A comprehensive invitation to tender, accompanied by an equally comprehensive statement of requirements, had been sent to potential suppliers and a shortlist drawn up on the basis of a number of weighted criteria. My memory tells me there were two suppliers on the shortlist: International Air Radio Ltd (IAL), who had supplied the Pilot System and Univac. The former was the preferred choice of my boss before the final evaluation had taken place; however, fate was to intervene.

I returned to the office after lunch one day and was met by nothing but very sad faces. The boss had gone out to lunch with his secretary at a local hotel and had suffered a fatal heart attack. The question of the succession arose, and despite my relatively recent arrival, I decided to throw my cap in the ring. My leading rival was also relatively new to the Metropolitan Police, just some six months before I joined, and he got the job.

Naturally, therefore, there was tension between us, and this was exacerbated by two issues. He apparently favoured Univac, whereas I was content to await the judgement of the evaluation. His preference was perhaps indicated by the summary he wrote for the final evaluation of tenders report. After stating the results of the evaluation, which were in favour of Univac, he added something to the effect that, in any case, they were a well-respected company. Although I agreed with the choice of Univac, I was not prepared to agree to such subjective comments being added after we had gone through such an objective evaluation. I likened it to a criminal trial in which the Defendant was bang to rights, but the Jury, on giving a "guilty" verdict added, "he looks a right villain anyway". Others, particularly the Police members of the team, agreed with me, and his words were deleted.

The second issue was concerning the security of the system. The plan was for the central mainframe of the system to be located in New Scotland Yard alongside Victoria Street and therefore vulnerable to a single terrorist device, which would result in the whole system being brought down. I suggested that this be reviewed, but my new boss would not contemplate under any circumstances changes to the system because of its impact on timescales. Whilst I was sympathetic to reducing changes to the design specification, as shown by my handling of the pilot system, I felt that the security issue was of such importance that a slight delay, if indeed there was to be one, was not significant. Furthermore, a change at the design stage, where we were at, rather than once the system had been installed and particularly when it was operational, would be much more easily accommodated. This time I did not prevail.

Nevertheless, I settled down to a role of monitoring Univac's progress in executing their contract. This included chairing the monthly progress meeting with them. It also included a visit to the USA to visit the Univac plants, which were to produce the hardware. There were two, the main one being in Minneapolis-Saint Paul, where the mainframe 1100s that were the hub of the system were produced, and the second in Irvine, California, where the minicomputers which were to be used as the nodes in the network were manufactured.

The visit to the latter was particularly important because Univac had only just taken over the Irvine-based Varian Computers who produced the minicomputers. I was therefore interested to check that, in the takeover, the Varian personnel and their product knowledge and hence the support we would require for the Project had not been lost. To this end, I asked discrete questions of bar owners and estate agents (realtors) around the ex-Varian Plant. As a result, I was able to determine that the likelihood of our having that particular problem was remote.

The USA trip was also a chance to visit some US Police Forces that used Univac computers and learn from their experience. Amongst these was the Houston Texas Police Department, where I spent an interesting evening in a squad car patrolling the road to Galveston.

Another force I visited was that of the Commonwealth of Pennsylvania in Harrisburg. My visit coincided with graduation day at their Police Academy, and as a representative of Scotland Yard, I was asked by the Commissioner to say a few words to the assembled masses. Not wishing to be churlish, I uttered a few banalities, which seemed to go down well. By coincidence, while I was speaking, the Three Mile Island nuclear incident was occurring a few miles away.

The airline ticket I had been issued with to make the trip included several legs. I changed it without any extra charge as they were within the mileage tolerance to also include three or four more legs, including visiting my old FAA stamping ground at Atlantic City. I also changed the homeward leg from New York to Heathrow via Manchester, again incurring no extra charge.

Somehow the expenses department of the Met learnt of this and practically accused me of living it up on the taxpayer. It took me some time to point out that this was not the case as (a) the change of airline ticket had not cost the taxpayer any extra, (b) I had not claimed any extra expenses incurred taking the extra legs and (c) any time spent performing them I had taken as annual leave agreed beforehand. Indeed, one of the extra legs involved an industrial visit that had benefit for the Met, without any cost to them.

My position with the Met also involved my liaising with other UK police forces. One notable occasion was a visit to the Strathclyde Force. The Heathrow to Glasgow Airport shuttle was late, and the Police Sergeant who met and drove me into Central Glasgow suggested we make up time. I agreed and was sped along the M8 at 120mph with siren wailing.

Cars generally were a key feature of Police culture. Within the Met, every office of Commander rank and their civilian equivalent had access to an official car and driver. Although just beneath that grade, I had access to the one dedicated to the project team. Here I must confess to having a conscience about potentially using a public asset for private use. For example, after a weekend in Manchester, I would have the car meet me off the train at Euston on Monday mornings.

Another key feature of the Police culture was drinking. It appeared to me that the Policemen I encountered were either teetotal Presbyterians or near or actual alcoholics. The latter's necessity for drink tended to be facilitated by many pubs and clubs in Central London letting you drink on the house if they knew you were the Met. Also, after a meeting in a Senior Policeman's office in the yard, it seemed a tradition for a desk drawer to be opened revealing bottles of whisky, particularly Johnnie Walker. One of these would then be opened and the contents shared.

One was also conscious that the Met, being always in the public eye, was constantly aware of its image. I was once lecturing to a group on a course at the Police College at Bramshill in Hampshire. My topic was IT systems procurement. I pointed out that there was no substitute for having as much information as possible on the individuals and organisations one was dealing with. As an afterthought, I added that I kept little back books with notes to that end. After my lecture, I was waylaid in a corridor by a livid Deputy Assistant Commissioner who had been interviewed on the BBC's Panorama programme the previous evening and had assured the public that the Met did not keep secret files on anyone. Nothing, however, came of my innocent indiscretion.

However, all this was background to my main focus of getting Univac to meet the system specification to time and budget. My strategy, as when dealing with any contractor to the public sector, was to be firm yet fair and always conscious of their commercial needs, albeit not to the detriment of the public and particularly its purse. My dealings with Univac were exactly the same; nevertheless, the sales department of Univac took exception to some of my actions and appeared to attempt to undermine me. This took the form of briefing the new deputy chief engineer that I had been bad-mouthing him to them.

Despite the tension that existed between us, this was simply not true. What was true was that he was too close, in my opinion, to Univac, as revealed by his proposed wording for the evaluation report. Nevertheless, the situation was clearly untenable and, despite the pleadings of the chief engineer, I moved on after less than two years.

Viewed retrospectively, transferring from one civil service bureaucracy bound organisation, NATS, to another, the Met, was not a sensible move. Not least, the former experience had probably left me with an attitude problem that did not help the situation.

CHAPTER 15

SALESMAN

My employment with the CAA and then the Metropolitan Police gave me a significant portfolio of contacts in the aviation and emergency services sectors. I was thus a potentially attractive acquisition for IT suppliers bidding in those marketplaces. I was consequently approached by Software Sciences Ltd of Farnborough with a view to joining their sales team, and given my difficulties with the Metropolitan Police and the public sector generally, I accepted.

Perhaps naively dazzled by the prospects of the gross salary I could earn with sales commissions, I agreed a rather low salary for my experience. Also, I was not happy when the promised company car turned out to be second-hand. Driving around in a second-hand car did not particularly trouble me, but what did was the signal it gave to me that Software Sciences were somewhat cynical in their treatment of their employees.

I commenced work with Software Sciences in February 1981 and immediately concentrated my sales effort on the CAA, who I knew were soon to go out to tender for three significant, in size and value, real time system turnkey contracts. These were, in chronological order:

MARETS, which was designed to be a sub-system to the UK's main air traffic control system allowing flight plans to be entered from military airfields.

SIRS, which was a system for displaying general information on the suites at the London Air Traffic Control Centre (LATCC).

EDDUS, which allowed controllers to input and amend flight plans directly from the LATCC suites. Effectively this was a permanent replacement to the lash up system for performing this function, which I alluded to in a previous chapter.

The first two contracts had a capital value of less than a million pounds, whereas EDDUS came in at about four million pounds. Unfortunately, there were obstacles to Software Sciences being invited to tender for these projects, let alone being awarded them. The company was currently implementing the North Atlantic Oceanic System, and not only would the CAA be reluctant to award another large contract to the company whilst that was in progress, but also it was not going well. The relevant CAA officers were accordingly not favourably disposed to giving Software Sciences any new work. I therefore conceived what I termed a "penance" curve. This was that the Company would be excluded from bidding for MARETS, would be allowed to bid for SIRS though unlikely to awarded it, and finally would be seriously considered for EDDUS.

I invited Bill Codner, the then director of data processing of NATS/CAA, to lunch in an Italian Restaurant in High Holborn and put the penance curve concept to him, albeit not in so many words. He went along with this, and given that SIRS and EDDUS were some time in the future, this allowed me in the short term to concentrate on other sales opportunities.

One of these was for a European Maritime system to be sited in Antwerp, and it was on a return Sabena flight from there that I became aware of a severe pain in my back passage. Alone in my flat in Ealing, the pain got worse, and my health rapidly deteriorated, so I had to summon help from my brother John. He arrived from Manchester, and although the local general practitioner had dismissed it as haemorrhoids, we realised something was seriously wrong, and he accompanied me to Accident and Emergency at Ealing General Hospital.

My condition was diagnosed as a fistula with internal complications necessitating an operation and subsequent two-week hospitalisation, followed by a lengthy convalescence with daily visits from the district nurse.

This was hardly a good start to my new career in sales. It also meant that I could not use my ticket for the FA Cup semi-final at Villa Park between City and Ipswich, which City won. I did, however, recover sufficiently to attend the cup final at Wembley, where City's opposition was Tottenham. The match was a draw, but more significantly, my attendance put back my recovery, and I was again too ill to attend the replay, which Tottenham won. Their winning goal by Ricardo Villa has been played ad nauseam on the television since, and viewing it pains me in both senses, particularly as Tottenham only got a replay because of a lucky equalizing own goal!

More significantly, I received a delightful get well card from a Rosemary Fleetwood. Rosemary was a divorced friend of my brother's who I had taken out to dinner the previous Christmas as my brother felt she needed cheering up. I had thought nothing of it at the time, but the card really touched my heartstrings.

Upon return to work, I concentrated on the police computer systems market. Generally, the police had a need for two types of real time systems; command and control and crime intelligence. There were and still are 52 separate police forces in the UK, and hence there was a market for approximately one hundred systems.

The cut-throat competition between the at least half a dozen companies, including Software Sciences, competing in this market meant that profits were hard to come by, and it drove at least one company, SPL, to the wall.

Furthermore, although each force had different requirements, there was scope for standardisation, for example, non-urban forces. This only happened in one instance with Kent and Humberside going for a joint system.

Non-standardisation was actually encouraged by the scientific officers of the Home Office's Police Scientific Development Branch, who saw in each contract scope for experimentation rather than standardisation, irrespective of the cost to the taxpayer.

Rivalry between forces also played a part with, for example, the Chief Constable of Merseyside, Ken Oxford, openly voicing his negative views of Greater Manchester's system requirements, whilst their Chief Constable, the "I talk to God" James Anderton, reciprocated.

This cutthroat nature of the marketplace did not dissuade Software Sciences from actively pursuing it, and I handled their bid for the Durham Constabulary criminal intelligence system. This I did assiduously making many trips to Durham. These included one winter's day in atrocious weather conditions, with the snow creating a whiteout as I sped north through the Vale of York on the 7 am train from Kings Cross. Amazingly, Software Sciences admonished me for not driving up and back in a day in my company car.

It appeared my efforts were paying off when the Durham Constabulary leaked their budget for the project to me, and I was able to persuade Software Sciences to bid within the budget, even though the "production department estimated" the costs were at least thirty percent higher. The deadline for the tenders was on a Monday morning, and in order to ensure they arrived safely, I went up to Manchester for the weekend and hand-delivered them in Durham on the Sunday. This was after a drama on the Saturday morning when I discovered a major error on the financial page of the tender, which had gone unspotted in the proofreading before I left Farnborough. Fortunately, I discovered a secretarial/printing company in Manchester, which enabled me to correct the tender documents there and then.

After all these efforts, my disappointment when the contract was awarded to one of our rivals, CAP, can be imagined. It seemed that their bid was lower than ours, despite the discount I had negotiated, and some years later, I learnt that, nevertheless, CAP made money on the contract.

Although I was not handling it, at the same time, Software Sciences were bidding for what became the notorious London Ambulance System. They did not succeed, but information via my colleague who was handling it indicated that it was a disaster in the making. My colleague had been involved in similar ambulance system projects in Witwatersrand in South Africa and in Devon and Cornwall, all of which had in common a common chief executive who ignored sensible advice, never mind good practice. Interestingly, this never came out in the inquiry and report into the London Ambulance System disaster.

I also pursued other sales opportunities, the most significant of which was for weather radar systems. This came about because of an advertisement in a European Journal for tenders to the Finnish Meteorological Office to put a weather radar system on the back of an existing Russian supplied radar.

A little research revealed that the world's most advanced weather radar system had been developed at the Royal Signals and Radar Establishment for the UK Meteorological Office. Interestingly, a system was already in operation using a radar in the Rossendale Hills, north of Manchester, with displays at several locations, including Manchester Airport. Discussions with the Meteorological Office gained their agreement that Software Sciences could offer this software as part of a tender package, and I therefore started to court the Finns. This involved visiting the radar site on the Russian border in the north of Finland with the result that every time I hear music by Sibelius, I remember long drives north from Helsinki through endless pine forests.

It quickly became apparent that weather radar systems was a market that was opening up, and soon I was handling on behalf of Software Sciences' bid for the Portuguese Meteorological Office. However, unlike the Finnish situation, the Portuguese required the radar as well. We therefore attempted to set up a bid consortium with Plessey, who seemed interested, but then withdrew from leadership of the consortium (they had the lion's share of the work) at the last minute, despite the possible income that could flow from being the first in this market. Undaunted, however, Software Sciences went ahead with Plessey as a sub-contractor.

Meanwhile, the tenders for the two Civil Aviation Authority Projects became due. Although on the basis of the penance curve Software Sciences could not hope to win the first, SIRS, clearly it was politic to put in a comprehensive bid for the second, MARETS, and this we did. We, of course, did not get the contract, but we then put significant effort into bidding for the EDDUS contract, not only because we had been promised an even playing field but also because of its much greater value.

Our efforts were nearly in vain. The tender deadline was 10 am on a Monday morning, and I set off early from my Ealing flat for the CAA offices in High Holborn. The journey was a direct one via the Central Line, and I had never experienced any problems before, but on this occasion, my tube broke down at White City where we stuck, not moving for over an hour, and I missed the deadline by some fifteen minutes.

Nevertheless, the tender was accepted, and eventually, we were successful. An early indication that this was to be the case came when we took the relevant Civil Aviation Authority personnel out to lunch at an Italian Restaurant in Drury Lane after making our final sales presentations. Most of the CAA personnel attending were my old colleagues, and they proceeded to pull my leg at every opportunity. As one of my Software Sciences colleagues perceptively pointed out, they would not have been that cruel if we had not secured the contract.

The euphoria of winning the contract and the resulting commission were soon, however, more than overshadowed by the death of my father. He had not been well for some time and became really ill whilst on holiday in Bournemouth with my mother. He was briefly hospitalised there, and I then drove down to Bournemouth when he was discharged and drove them both back to Manchester. He was obviously in a very bad way, and my abiding memory of the day was a late evening sunset as we drove north and his words when we arrived in Manchester – "I knew the big lad would get me home".

The next day, concerned about his condition, I stayed in the North and went to work at Software Sciences Macclesfield office. During the day, his condition worsened, and he was admitted to North Manchester General Hospital, fifteen minutes walk from the old family home. Such was his condition that my mother and I were allowed to stay with him, but as it approached midnight, I suggested she go home, which she did.

Some hours later, Father passed away, and I drove through a wild, wet, windy night to the sheltered accommodation where my parents then lived to break the news to Mother. Both of us were comforted by Rosemary, who by then was my girlfriend, and she then attempted to get in touch with my brother, who was touring the USA. Eventually, she located him in Las Vegas, from where he flew straight home. I felt guilty because I had advised him on the telephone a few days earlier that Father's condition was not so severe that he needed to fly home.

A couple of days after the funeral, I set off to drive back to London via Wiltshire to drop off my Auntie Bertha and Uncle Jack, who had attended the funeral. However, no doubt through stress, partway down the motorway, I started to feel distinctly unwell. I therefore dropped my aunt and uncle at Birmingham New Street Station so they could continue their journey by train whilst I returned to Manchester.

It was a week before I felt well enough to return to London and Software Sciences, where I found all hell had broken loose over the Portuguese Weather System project. Portuguese protocol for foreign companies tendering for public centre contracts required tenders to be issued via the embassy of the company's country. I had therefore primed the Commercial Attaché at the British embassy in Lisbon to expect the invitation to tender and to send it on to us.

It had arrived whilst I was in Manchester, and the Attaché, rather than sending it by mail, chose to put it in a diplomatic bag for the Foreign Office in London. However, it was designated as low priority compared to the regular diplomatic mail, and as the bag was continually full, it was regularly excluded, so it was some days before it was sent. It then languished for several days at the Foreign Office, despite my strenuous attempts to locate it when I returned.

Software Sciences had not helped, with the person designated to handle things in my absence showing no initiative to expedite matters, as obviously he would not receive any commission for it, whereas he had other priorities, for which he would. Eventually, when we did receive it, it was not possible to respond in time, which was particularly galling, as I had negotiated sole supplier status for Software Sciences.

Software Sciences and I had similar bad luck with the bid for the Finnish contract. We were on the shortlist, along with the Swedish giant Ericsson, and unfortunately, whilst the tenders were being evaluated, all the Nordic countries devalued in sync, making our bid financially uncompetitive compared to Ericsson's.

The stress of working for Software Sciences was infinitely greater than the public sector environment of the Civil Aviation Authority and the Metropolitan Police. At the London Air Traffic Control Centre, for example, it was daily practice to retire to the canteen for mid-morning and afternoon tea. Although this had benefits in terms of networking with one's colleagues, it was hardly conducive to a dynamic environment.

At Software Sciences, on the contrary, there were no such luxuries and life was made even more fraught by a lack of organisation and a culture of short-termism. For example, in preparing complex tender documents, one had to scrounge typing facilities from wherever one could. On one occasion, I was travelling almost hourly between the three Farnborough sites to collate a document, the typing of which was spread between the three. Another example was the withdrawal, with no notice, of my support team for the Weather Radar software so they could be allocated to body shop work for clients, which offered a no-risk immediate return.

Although obviously not necessarily typical, the experience did indicate some generalisations between working in the public sector – too easy and the private sector – too frenetic. What I did learn the practical hard way from my Software Sciences experience was effective sales and marketing, which proved more than useful when I later set up my own company.

Also, I had now worked on both sides of the customer/supplier fence for IT services, and this gave me a unique insight into the issues from both sides perspectives.

However, this work pressure, plus the dearth of my social life, which exacerbated the depressive effect of living alone in a flat in Ealing, coupled with the death of my father, conspired to significantly impact my mental health. As well as becoming depressed, I suffered serious anxiety attacks. One of these was whilst changing flights in Copenhagen, where I became almost unable to get myself on my connecting flight because of mental confusion.

Things became so bad that one evening I contacted the Samaritans from my flat. Software Sciences were no help, although I may not have articulated the severity of my condition to them, but it was obvious that I could not go on working in that environment. However, I hung on until the first significant payments for the EDDUS project had been made to Software Sciences, and I had my significant commission in my bank account. Then I handed in my notice. I did not have a job to go to even if I had been able to perform one, but then the EDDUS commission provided a financial cushion.

CHAPTER 16

CROSSROADS

Some years before, my brother and I had purchased 91 Hazelbottom Road in Manchester on behalf of our parents, who were the sitting tenants. They had subsequently moved out into sheltered accommodation, but my brother had remained living there, and I used it as my Manchester base.

My brother had gone about renovating it with us sharing the funding, but with a marriage on the horizon, he was ready to move out, so it seemed sensible for me to move back north and live there. I therefore sold my apartment in Ealing, which I also had purchased as a sitting tenant. Both sitting tenant purchases had been on significantly advantageous financial terms. However, if I had known about the imminent boom in London property prices, I would not have sold the flat and would have reaped an even greater financial return.

Meanwhile, I was, of course, unemployed and in the much more lenient climate of those days managed to sustain a case that I had been constructively dismissed by Software Sciences by virtue of their treatment of me. I was, therefore, immediately entitled to the dole.

The person in the local employment office who initially handled it, in view of the significant sum, particularly the EDDUS commission that I had already earned that year, treated my initial request with some scepticism. Nevertheless, it was established that I was entitled to it, modest as it was.

As a result of the rest and removing myself from London, my mental health began to improve with the significant assistance of Dr Bhisma, the family general practitioner, who later became a firm friend. Rather than suggesting that I had some acute psychological problem, he diagnosed that I was just mentally worn out. This diagnosis was important to me as, given how I had exited my four employments, I was beginning to wonder whether the employment problems I had encountered were the result of my own paranoia.

Another major factor in my recovery was the support of Rosemary. Eventually, she moved in with me at 91, with us jointly buying out my brother's share, who by then had got married.

Rosemary had been divorced for a number of years and remarkably had brought up three daughters on her own whilst also working and getting a degree as a mature student once they had grown up. In a letter I sent her before leaving London, I described her as brainy, determined and elegantly beautiful. This was not flattery and was indeed an understatement, and she proved to be the best thing that ever happened to me.

The three daughters, by the time Rosemary moved in with me, were all around twenty years old, and although all three spent some time living with us, they soon moved off as they got careers and/ or married. Rosemary's only other close relative with whom she was in contact was her father, the Reverend Stanley Meadows. He introduced me to the Manchester Pedestrians, allegedly the world's oldest gentlemen's walking club, and I soon joined. The regular Saturday of walks with them in the northern countryside followed by pub dinners was a further contributor to my recovery.

Another contributor was becoming a regular attendee at St Thomas's Church, the one I had attended as a Child. I had never been a great believer and did not become one then;, however, it was very therapeutic to effectively go through the motions of belief.

My involvement also enabled me to use my organisational talents in support of the Church community and eventually become Church Warden. This required a significant amount of my time involved with the Church, as described later in Chapter 25. I also spent some of my time writing a book on managing computer projects based on my experience up to that time. This was eventually published and sold nearly two thousand copies.

However, any income from sales of the book was a long way off, and the dole hardly supported my lifestyle, so not wishing to eat up all my Software Sciences commission, nor the proceeds from the sale of my London apartment, I considered my future options.

Initially, I toyed with doing something completely different, like opening or buying a wine/piano bar, but, eventually, I decided this cobbler should stick to his last. I therefore decided to stay working in Information Technology (IT) but, given my track record in employment, decided I would work on a freelance basis. To this end, I formed my own company, aided by £40 per week from a government "Enterprise Allowance" scheme. My sense of ownership dictated my own name should appear in the name of the company. Also, I wanted to offer advice on projects, so, following discussions with my friends Sheila and Denys Moody whilst staying with them down in St Mawgan in Cornwall, I settled on the name Price Project Services.

Sheila and Denys owned the Old Rectory there, a grade two listed building, and staying there, adjacent to the spectacular North Cornish coast, including Watergate Bay and Bedruthan Steps, was a further factor in my recuperation.

This was in April 1984, and initially, I did some freelance jobs via an agency. However, government tax changes dictated that you could only work through an agency if you were a limited company, so in November of that year, I changed the company's status to limited. Hitherto, it had been a sole tradership. Price Project Services Ltd

(PPSL), as it became, had a hundred shares, ninety-five of which were in my name and five in Rosemary's, who was officially the company secretary.

Incidentally, many years later, the government tax rules changed again so that freelancers working for one client could no longer act as a limited company with the advantages that status bestowed. However, by that time, PPSL had several clients/assignments at once and its own premises and employed people, so I did not have to revert to being a sole trader.

The sales and marketing experience with Software Sciences was of obvious use in my new venture. Particularly, rather than waiting for work to come to me, I knew how to go out and seek it. This was just as well as despite my extensive contacts, they did not prove useful in providing me with revenue-earning assignments.

Also, I soon noticed an interesting phenomenon that assignments generally arrived from unexpected quarters and not from the sources where one had concentrated one's sales and marketing. However, if one did not put one's back into sales and marketing, even these unexpected assignments failed to materialise.

There was, however, one aspect of running a company where I was illequipped: financial management. I therefore took advantage of the considerable advice that was available from government sources, banks, etc, on how to start up a company. With the benefit of hindsight, I feel that a lot of what was then on offer, and possibly still is, was rather naïve. For example, one of the first recommendations to anyone starting up in business is to get yourself an accountant.

My own advice now would be that you need to fulfil three roles to provide the necessary financial advice to a company. These are bookkeeper, auditor and financial adviser. Although some accountants may provide all three, most only serve to be bookkeepers and auditors, and rather than being financial advisers, they are simply servants of the taxman.

Initially, I did my own bookkeeping, but later I paid my brother as a part-time employee to do it. Doing it myself had its advantages. Firstly it gave me a hands-on feel for how the company was doing financially whilst being careful to differentiate between my own and the company's monies.

Secondly, it made me appreciate the financial governance obligations that are placed on companies in the UK and the time one has to spend dealing with their absurd complexities, particularly the three forms of taxation: Corporation, Value Added (VAT) and, despite its name, National Insurance.

Naturally, I usually paid myself dividends rather than a salary, thus legitimately avoiding paying National Insurance Contributions as both an employer and employee. However, every three years, I reverted to paying myself a salary to avoid capping what I could pay into my pension fund. Maximum pension contributions in the UK were linked directly to salary levels.

My financial obligations were such that I could support my lifestyle from the dividend payments I allowed myself or from my salary when I paid myself one, in the latter case, without venturing into the higher tax bands.

Subject to the above constraint, I therefore paid as much money as possible into the company pension funds as insurance for my old age.

Without realising it, I accidentally furthered my future pension by not opting out of the state pension scheme, even though I had set up the company scheme thus maximising the state pension I received when I came to retire. Most company pension schemes require employees to opt out of the state scheme when they join a company scheme, and as a result, they only receive the basic state pension, plus what they get from the employer's scheme. I was therefore lucky that my inadvertent decision meant I got a state pension linked to my significant salary payments and not the basic amount.

Complex as these financial considerations were, they could have been far worse.

Consultancy, which is what I was offering, required no significant capital outlays for me to start and continue trading, so I avoided having to seek loans from banks or elsewhere, with all the hassle and stress that involved. Even in the early days, the money I had saved from my Software Sciences commission and the sale of my London apartment was sufficient to pay my limited start-up costs and tide me over until income exceeded expenditure. The Enterprise Allowance also helped. Even the VAT system onto which I had to enrol when the company's turnover exceeded the threshold, at which it had to sign up, proved beneficial.

My eventual clients were mainly government departments, large corporations and the like who could claim back the VAT I charged them and therefore, it was not an issue in my obtaining work from them. At the same time, my company was able to get back any VAT it was charged for its supplies, reducing their costs significantly.

Given these factors, I cannot claim that my sally into entrepreneurship was as risky as it might have been. However, it still meant I had to monitor:

- Was there enough possible work I could do?
- Was I in a position to profitably bid for it?
- Were sufficient of these bids successful?
- Did I do the work to the reasonable satisfaction of the clients?
- Was I invoicing them in a timely manner?
- Were they paying in a timely manner?

By applying this checklist regularly, I ensured that apart from on a few occasions, I never ran into cash flow problems.

CHAPTER 17

AGENCY WORK

Initially, I was not certain what was PPSL offering; in the words of Oscar Wilde, "I have nothing much to declare except my genius". I therefore, in the early years of the company, mostly worked as a freelancer through an agency, PE Computer Services.

In this capacity, I undertook a number of assignments, one of the first of which was for the Aintree, Liverpool based Vernons organisation. Vernons were and are mostly known for running football pools in the UK.

However, less well known was that they ran lotteries for various companies and states around the world. Increasingly though, such lotteries required a computer system to support them, and if they were to stay in the market, Vernons required such a system. They had decided to develop such a system themselves, but the project had run into trouble, and my task was to investigate why.

One reason I soon discovered was that responsibility for the project was split between two disparate parts of the company's organisation. The central computer system was being produced by the computer department, whereas the remote terminals were being produced by the engineering function within the organisation. The two parts of the organisation only came together at Chief Executive Officer level, and there was no interface mechanism at a lower level.

My report, which was the outcome of the assignment, made recommendations to remedy this and other deficiencies and seemed to be well received. Apart from the work, the highlight for me was a lunchtime walk around the adjacent Grand National racecourse.

A further assignment was for British Nuclear Fuels Ltd (BNFL) at Birchwood, Warrington. BNFL were building the THORP nuclear reprocessing facility at Windscale in Cumbria. My task was to write the computer operating standards for THORP, which is what I did. Interestingly, I was never invited to THORP, which might have been useful.

My next assignment was further afield for International Computers Ltd (ICL) in Euston Road, London. This London location close to Euston station was convenient, as the task necessitated commuting up to London three days a week for several weeks.

The task was an investigation into the effectiveness of an investment programme in marketing projects. It included reviewing the procedures for the monitoring of progress and financial control of the various projects within the investment programme. My outputs were reports on the current status of the programme and recommendations for the ongoing project management procedures. My marketing and sales experience with Software Sciences proved extremely useful in doing this.

There was one assignment where the client was not happy with what I had done. The client was Kingston Communications Ltd in Hull on Humberside. Kingston Communications had an interesting history. Hull had its own telephone exchange, which was the only municipal telephone exchange in the UK that had not become absorbed in organisational terms into the national network. Subsequently, the Hull local authority privatised the organisation as the limited company, Kingston Communications. Apart from fulfilling its standard telecommunications function, the company was seeking to expand into new areas, one of which was to become a systems house. My task was to produce the standards for the systems house in conjunction with a junior colleague who was also a freelancer. My role was to produce the systems analyst part of the standards, whereas my colleague was tasked with producing the programming part of the standards.

The brief was to base them on the SSADM (Structured Systems Analysis and Design Method) methodology, which I felt had weaknesses. I therefore produced a set of standards, which improved, in my opinion, the basic SSADM offering. Despite my explanations of what I had done and why, the Kingston Communications Computer Manager wanted the risk-averse approach of a bog-standard SSADM offering, and thus was critical of what I produced. A further exacerbating problem was the difficult attitude of my colleague. The outcome was that I modified what I had produced to make it acceptable but without charge for the extra work.

As I recount later, by the late nineteen eighties, my marketing and sales were starting to generate work for PPSL direct without the need for an agency. Soon I was therefore able to do without any agency work, but first, I performed two assignments at North West Water.

North West Water, like all the UK water companies, was about to be privatised, and as a precursor, all its operations were being scrutinised. This scrutiny revealed that its computer development team, some sixty strong, had not produced a new system for over a decade. Two tiers of the relevant managers had therefore been shown the door, and my first assignment was to act as locum manager until permanent replacements could be recruited.

I was contracted for three days a week, but I found even this was excessive. My modus operandi, which I had used previously, was to have weekly minuted meetings with the project leaders. At each meeting, I checked their objectives for the next week and, at the following one, checked whether they had been met. This enabled me to assess progress and the ability of the project leaders to achieve it.

It was interesting that one project leader spent most of his time attempting to justify lack of progress rather than achieving it. I noted this in the report for my permanent successors on all of the staff. It was with surprise, therefore, when I later learnt that this individual had not only retained his position but had been promoted.

My second stint at North West Water was to carry out a strategic study into the Systems Development Department's use of methodologies and Computer-Aided Software Engineering (CASE) tools and make recommendations for an integrated future strategy for both to meet the Authority's long-term business objectives. I also defined a framework for all-embracing IT (Computer and Communications) management and technical standards.

Although not in my original plan working through an agency was a useful transition from full-time employment to entrepreneurship.

CHAPTER 18

SHEFFIELD WEDNESDAY

About a year after I had set up PPSL, Reay Elliott told me that Universities were looking out for experienced individuals, like myself, to teach their students. Reay was the Industrial Training Officer at Brunel University who had supplied my CAA team with students in the 1970s. So I sent my details to the Computer Science departments of a number of universities within range of Manchester. Sheffield University responded by offering me a part-time role lecturing to Masters Students on Software Engineering.

My duties initially consisted of giving ten one hour lectures to masters students and setting and marking tutorial and examination questions. However, this only lasted for the first year because, subsequently, Sheffield involved me in a unique way of "teaching" the software engineering component of computer science.

Professor Mike Holcombe and (now Doctor) Hugh Lafferty were pioneering students' learning by them performing a real life computer project, with, most critically, the students working in teams. They had developed four variants of this approach, the most severe of which was for students taking a four-year undergraduate course leading to a masters in engineering.

These students were not only expected to perform the technical part of their projects but were also expected to handle all the commercial elements of the project, including creating a legally constituted company under which banner the project was conducted.

Another variant, termed the MAXI Project, was for students taking a conventional masters course. They were only charged with performing the technical aspects of the project, although this included the investigation of the feasibility of the project and the formulation of the requirements.

To achieve the realism of the project, a client who required a computer system was required, as well as a manager for the project. For the first year, Hugh Lafferty performed both these roles, as well as lecturing to the students. This was hardly realistic, and after the first year, they realised that the project manager was a role I was almost ideally suited for. They also found independent clients who had a requirement for a computer system to perform that role.

This was to be my involvement with Sheffield University for some twenty years, in which time over 1300 students undertook the MAXI with approximately fifty different user projects – in a typical year, there might be three users with several student teams addressing each user's needs.

Although I could make no claim to the idea, which was solely Mike's and Hugh's, the concept had my full support, and I could claim that as far as the MAXI was concerned, how it was implemented was primarily down to me.

Team size was the first consideration and the ideal, based on organisational theory, appeared to be five students, although sometimes the number of students meant some teams had only four or three members.

Despite my reservations about it, the projects were planned using the waterfall model of software development with five distinct stages. This happily meant each student had a shot at being stage manager responsible for the planning and execution of each stage. The use of the waterfall model with every team executing each stage in the same timescale as the other teams was largely dictated by my own needs. Teams providing me with the same outputs but on widely varying dates would have made my task, particularly marking, very difficult, if not impossible.

Initially, the University required that the projects used SSADM, which, as I indicated previously, I also had significant reservations about. These were, to my mind, vindicated in relation to the feasibility stage of the projects very soon after I started managing the MAXI. I was marking the feasibility study reports one night on the train returning to Manchester from London. I commented on Team A's efforts "you have not addressed feasibility", similarly for Team B, then Team C, then Team D. Soon, I began to doubt whether all the students could get it wrong, so I consulted the SSADM manual, and it turned out feasibility was scarcely mentioned even though the methodology was supposed to address it.

The University also required that the projects use the PRINCE project management methodology. I had no problems with this because I considered PRINCE a packaged aggrandisement of routine and simple project management procedures that many, including myself, had been using for years. These procedures included reviewing a project at the end of each stage. I did cut back on this because whatever the outcome of the feasibility study, the students would be proceeding with the projects anyway, and therefore, there was little point in making the proceed/don't proceed decision, which forms a key part of a stage review, in the feasibility review.

I also dispensed with the implementation and testing stage reviews. As they were too near the end of the project to really influence the outcome, they therefore did not justify spending my limited time on them. I felt that the two reviews at the end of the requirements and design stages, which I did conduct, were sufficient to appraise the students with what was involved.

The scheduling of the various stages of the projects was also a problem. The students, like many so-called computer scientists, were keen to start programming as soon as possible, whereas I was determined to ensure they had really sorted out the requirements and design before features became relatively too embedded in the software. Unfortunately, in an ideal world, this would have meant them starting programming just before the long Christmas break, and I was concerned about them stopping and starting programming. Therefore, I delayed the start of the implementation phase until they returned for the spring term.

Also, a later start was more compatible with their teaching schedule, and it avoided me asking them to do things before they were formally taught by the computer science department academics. These factors made the students MAXI work more hectic in spring term, but I had to point out that it would have been more hectic if they had to rework programs because of a requirements and design that was not firm.

Another complication was that I encouraged the students to formally review their work before finalising it, as occurred in real life. To this end, I required them to submit draft feasibility, requirements and design to me, and I would participate in their formal reviews of these documents. This meant when I came to mark these documents, I was, to a degree, partially marking my own performance, as well as that of the students.

The MAXI programme I drew up for the students at the start of the academic year included the start and end dates of each stage, the latter indicating when the products of the stage had to be handed in or, in the case of the programming, the product being reviewed.

Before the former, the stage manager had to hand in a detailed plan for the stage, which he or she had agreed with team colleagues. The programme also indicated when draft deliverables for reviewing were to be handed in and the dates of their review. It also showed when I would brief them on what was required in each stage. These briefings were given to the whole class, whereas all my other contacts with the students, including reviews, were through tutorials with each team.

The former lasted about half an hour, whereas the latter typically lasted about twenty minutes, except one year when there were something like seventy-five students - this was reduced to fifteen minutes with a revolving door policy. Normally, the MAXI involved my visiting the university some fifteen times over the autumn and spring terms during which the MAXI was conducted. Obviously, there were some weeks when I felt it was unnecessary for me to see the student teams, and it was better for them to carry on under their own initiative.

The programme was given to the students as one of the documents supporting the briefing for the MAXI Project, which I gave students at the start of the autumn term. This was combined with the Stage 1, Feasibility Study briefing. However, before these two briefings, I gave the students a lecture on software engineering, which was a condensation of the ten lectures I had given in my first year teaching at Sheffield.

The combined briefings and lecture took about three hours with one short break, but these were not the only tasks I undertook on this first day. The students had to be divided up into teams, and for the first two or three years, this was done in a sophisticated way to ensure each team, where possible, had a mix of students who together had the range of skills and experience required by the MAXI. This was done on the basis of the information provided to the University when the students applied.

However, this seemed to produce no more tangible benefits than picking the teams at random, so this was what was done for later years.

Then I left it to the academic staff, and I believe the only criterion they used was to ensure that each team contained at least one student who had English as his or her first language, as increasingly the class contained more and more foreign students.

The other non-lecturing task I undertook was to meet the users. This gave me an opportunity to brief them on what they had to provide to the students and the dates to which the students and they had to work. I made it clear that unless there were severe problems, which cropped up only occasionally over the years, they should only liaise with the students and not me. The most important part of this liaison was for the user to agree with each team their requirements and sign off the report documenting them.

This meant that although the requirements report might comprise the SSADM features, it must also contain a narrative version the user could comprehend.

After this initial burst of activity, my work on the MAXI settled down to weekly visits to Sheffield to conduct stage briefings, review of stage deliverables, end-of-stage reviews and routine progress meetings. I also gave short ad-hoc lectures on specific topics relevant to the MAXI, e.g. risk management. These weekly visits normally occupied an afternoon with me doing any necessary preparatory work on the train between Manchester and Sheffield.

However, when I was down to conduct a document review, this would occupy a whole day with the morning spent reading the draft student documents ready for the afternoon review with the students.

I was also responsible for marking the MAXI. This had two constituent parts. Firstly I marked the outputs from each stage, for example, the feasibility study and test plan. Then in conjunction with the user, who allocated marks relevant to his or her perspective, I marked the final product in all its aspects, including a User Manual.

The balance of marks between the stages and final product was such that, in theory, a team could have no marks for the stages, but if their final product was brilliant, they might to just scrape a pass. This was consistent with an emphasis on product rather than process. In fact, this never happened, and almost always, the teams that excelled at the stages generally produced the better final products.

For me, the most difficult aspect in the marking and in the MAXI generally was allocating marks to individual students within a team. In the early years, the individual student mark comprised the team mark, plus a potential twenty percent for him or her, depending on my assessment of their contribution. Later I increased this to thirty percent. I based my assessment of an individual students contribution on a number of factors:

- My own subjective observation of them in tutorials.
- Their performance in the role of Stage Manager.
- Indications of their contributions from the number of signed-off test specifications, pieces of code, etc, (they had to indicate authorship in comment statements), against their names.
- The number of hours of work contributed by each student to each stage – all members of a team had to jointly sign a document containing their hours. This idea was not my own but came from the other team project courses in the Computer Science Department.

Inevitably this was not perfect, but I strove to ensure no student who deserved to pass failed but some who deserved to fail passed. Perhaps predictably, controversy sometimes ensued. The most common one was that a team had produced a better product, in their opinion, than another team but had got a lower mark. However, quite often, I was able to point out that this was because the other team's product was more consistent with what they had promised in the signed-off requirements documents.

The remuneration from the University was considerably less than what I received for my commercial work. However, it was a regular income despite the University agonising each year over whether they had a budget for me and my never having any formal contractual arrangement with them. Because the University had a limited budget and could not reclaim VAT, rather than bill them through PPSL, I did it as an individual. Financially, things went smoothly except on one occasion when they unjustifiably started to apply tax to my expense claims. However, after discussions, a satisfactory way was found around this.

I also never had a formal title for my relationship with the University, although an early communication from them described me as an industrial fellow, and so that was the title I subsequently used when occasion demanded. The real motivation for my undertaking the work was the rather altruistic one that I felt I had something of value to pass on to the students. Most students seemed to share this view, judging by the comments I received when I entertained the students to drinks at the end of the MAXI.

Perhaps more independent and valid were the same views expressed by the two students who I had on industrial placement with PPSL as well as others with whom I became friendly, long after I had finished teaching them.

Most students felt that the most significant thing they learnt from the MAXI was team working, and it was the team aspect that gave me the greatest satisfaction and, retrospectively, greatest humour. The greatest satisfaction was the quality of work produced by a team comprising representatives from all five continents. The most humorous, although it presented me with significant student counselling problems, was provided by a team comprising three females and one male.

The guy got into an affair with Girl A, unbeknown to the other two girls. He then broke off with Girl A to her chagrin and started an affair with Girl B. She then found out that she was second choice to *her* chagrin. Finally, Girl C found out she had been totally left out, to *her* chagrin. Thereafter, my tutorials with the team were more than a little fraught, but to his credit, the guy did give me a written apology.

Over the years, the general characteristics of the students changed. Initially, many were effectively taking a conversion course from a first degree in a subject other than Computer Science. They were funded by the Manpower Services Commission (MSC), and I generally felt the standard was lower than that which I would expect from masters students at a Russell Group University (the upper echelon of UK universities). I therefore had to adjust my teaching and expectations accordingly.

Eventually, this MSC funding dried up, and increasingly the students were from overseas. The University had a link with the University of Thessalonica, and hence many of these overseas students came from Greece. Initially, they appeared to be playboys, just in the UK for a good time, but my subjective opinion was that as the years went on, they generally became more diligent.

However, one common factor was their male chauvinism, and one Chinese girl suffered terribly in a team of otherwise team of Greek males until I transferred her to another team.

Teaching overseas students meant I had to be careful to avoid English colloquialisms and particularly humour. Once in my initial lecture, I opined, "If you learn anything from me, it is that in a computer project, good requirements are paramount, and Manchester United are crap".

After the lecture, a female Chinese student came up to me and said, "I understand about requirements, but what is Manchester United and what is crap?"

The actual projects covered a variety of topics. One standby in early days, promoted by Hugh Lafferty, was a package for the management of a Swimming Gala, the fiendish complexity of which was such as to induce a dread of water commensurate with that produced by sharks.

Other projects included an expert system for playing contract bridge, a hacking tool, and a package to manage a dentists practice, complete with graphics showing a diagrammatic representation of a person's teeth and gums.

Very few, if any of the projects, were used operationally, but the students did not know this at the start, so I do not believe it detracted from their experience. For the users, even if they did not get an operational system, it was a learning experience that enabled them to be much more effective in implementing a future system.

Apart from one year, I attended the University on Wednesdays. This had the inconvenience of breaking up the week with resultant scheduling problems for my other assignments. However, it gave added significance to me of the term Sheffield Wednesday. For the first few years, I was entertained for lunch in the senior common room. Later, however, I was entertained after I finished in a local pub, the Red Deer.

Generally, I was so tired after my lectures and tutorials that rather than risk cross Pennine driving, particularly in winter, I took the train, which also allowed me to drink. One year, Hugh Lafferty became perplexed that, on presenting his bill for entertaining me to the University finance department, he was always paid around eighteen pounds, irrespective of the actual amount. After a while, it transpired the finance people were confusing the time of the bill with the amount.

I also made more modest contributions to the University. One was sitting on the Computer Science Department Industrial Liaison

Committee. Several were attempts to spread the learning through real life team project concepts further afield. This was relatively unsuccessful, with most academics elsewhere deciding it was too difficult!!

Leeds University did, however, institute something similar but with the disadvantage that the manager, user and academic roles were combined in one individual and not separate.

For my part, the teaching, as well as being a source of income and an outlet for my altruism, was beneficial to me in that it made me clarify and make more coherent my experience of computer projects in order to pass my experience on to the students.

Not all my teaching experiences were beneficial or indeed successful. Early in my independent career, I was recruited by the Learning Tree Company to present their four-day project management course. As a precursor, I had to sit in on one while one of their experienced teachers presented the course. They appeared to be in a hurry for me to start because the location they chose for me to do this was Washington DC.

Immediately on my return, I presented the course myself in London. This was not successful, partly because I was not comfortable simply presenting other people's material, unlike my Sheffield work or a course, again on project management, which I gave to the Plessey Group on behalf of the National Computing Centre where I presented my own material.

Another factor was that the Learning Tree course required me to include a section instructing the use of a project management package on a PC, where my lack of knowledge of the package and my poor keyboard skills were found out. Not surprisingly, the Learning Tree company did not employ me again.

Stan Price

CHAPTER 19

MONITOR

Sometime in 1985/86, I saw that the American Institute of Electrical and Electronic Engineering (IEEE), of which I was an associate member, had a meeting of its UK chapter at my old college, Kings. Furthermore, the title of the accompanying talk was "Software Engineering – Myth or Reality", or a similar title. This intrigued me, and I decided to attend. The speaker was a Professor A.C. Davies of City University, and he referenced the US Air Traffic Control Computer System, about which I was, of course, very knowledgeable. After the talk, I introduced myself to him and mentioned my involvement, and he asked what my current situation was. When I replied that I was looking for assignments, he advised that I could be of use to the Alvey Programme.

The Alvey Programme was a UK research initiative into new software technologies, with a budget of half a billion pounds. It was inspired by the Japanese Fifth Generation Initiative, which had similar objectives. Fearful that through it, the Japanese would achieve domination in the software sector as they had done in other sectors, including electronics and automobiles, the UK government had created the Alvey Programme in order to ensure the UK did not fall behind.

Alvey was run jointly by the UK Research Councils and Department of Trade and Industry (DTI), and Professor Davies gave me a person to contact in the latter. This was David Talbot, the director in the Alvey Programme responsible for Software Engineering. I immediately contacted David Talbot, and he informally interviewed me. The outcome was that I was given an assignment monitoring one of the research projects within the software engineering portfolio of the Alvey Programme. Monitoring basically consisted of periodically inspecting a project and reporting back to DTI and the Research Councils, but particularly the DTI, on how the project was proceeding, especially in meeting its research objectives and ensuring the taxpayer's money was not being wasted.

The projects were generally undertaken by a mixed industrial/ academic consortium with the taxpayers funding up to fifty percent of the costs via a grant. The academic partners were fully funded in this way, and what remained was split, with variable percentages, between the industrial partners. The academic partner in this first project was Edinburgh University, and the industrial partners were International Computers Ltd (ICL) and British Telecom (BT). Its subject matter was an integrated modelling support environment.

Although, at that time, there were some designated processes for monitoring, particularly endorsing the grant claims, generally, how one went about it was left to oneself. So I simply got on with it, and what I did must have been acceptable because I was soon offered more work monitoring other projects. These included some-where a previous monitoring officer had proved unsatisfactory. Eventually, I would monitor over sixty projects before I retired, with, at the peak, eleven projects simultaneously.

Surprisingly, most projects had a timescale of three years, despite the variations in their subject matter, scope and size and budgets in the hundreds of thousands to several million pounds. Most projects did not exist in isolation but were part of several research programmes, each with a different theme or objective, with Alvey being the first in which I was involved. The following chapter contains details of the more memorable programmes and projects and particularly their subject matter.

The detailed practice of monitoring to which I made a significant contribution involved, in the early days, checking the progress of the project monthly against a project plan they had prepared in advance and approved by the sponsors. Soon, however, the monitoring intervals were increased to quarterly, and although this meant less for me, I was quite sanguine as I felt it was a more cost-effective use of the taxpayer's money. The only significant exceptions to the general project timescale template described above were six projects, which were awarded grants in a programme specifically aimed at creativity. These grants were only of the order of £25,000 and with timescales of six months.

There were several ways I monitored the progress of a project, except in exceptional circumstances, on a monthly and then quarterly basis, dependant on the monitoring cycle. I was given visibility of the quality of the project's work by examining their deliverables. Many of these were reports, which were sent to me. Others were actual "products", often software, which usually required me to visit one of the project partners premises to see a demonstration of it. These visits, wherever possible, were combined with a monthly/quarterly meeting with the project team. In advance of these meetings, I required, and more often than not, got a report from the project. Before reading this, I drew up a list of questions for the project primarily based on where they should be according to their project plan. Any questions a report failed to answer, I then asked in the meeting. Following the meeting, I would then prepare a report for the DTI outlining my findings.

Inevitably some projects took exception to being monitored, especially if one was critical of them. The principal of one project actually questioned my ability to criticise his project as he was a world expert in its subject matter. My response that one needn't be an engine driver to recognise a train crash proved an effective riposte. Another retort I resorted to, although this time not my own, was when a project pleaded after I expressed concern about the time it was taking, "Hang on, Rome wasn't built in a day", was the standard, "I know. I was not on that project!"

Where the meetings were held determined my mode of travel. A few in Scotland and Northern Ireland and one in Devon meant flying, but my usual mode was by train. The central position of Manchester facilitated this, and as a railway buff, I, of course, had no objections. Travel by train also meant an effective use of my time, assuming the journey was long enough. On the outward journey, I would prepare my questions and then see if the project's report answered them and if not, I produced a list of those for the meeting plus any other points I needed to bring up. For example, what capital equipment had they purchased and were going to claim for. I used the homeward journey to prepare my report. Before I had a laptop, I drafted a paper version, which Rosemary subsequently typed but later, once I had a laptop, I prepared them myself.

Also, on the journey home, I checked the project's grant claims for the previous period. To facilitate this, I used a set of standard spreadsheets which one of my Sheffield students had written in the course of a work placement with PPSL.

When quarterly monitoring was introduced, it was assumed that two days a quarter would be sufficient for a three-partner project, with extensions if there were problems and/or the project had significantly more partners. Nevertheless, two days was extremely tight, and I found it only feasible if I worked one day a quarter attending the meeting and working on the train.

The other day was taken up finalising my reports and claims, reading document deliverables and answering queries from both the Project and the sponsors. In this, Rosemary helped me, but I did not charge for her time. It also helped when one was monitoring several projects at once as, for example, sometimes I could schedule meetings with different project teams on the same or adjacent days if they were geographically close.

Payment was on the basis of a daily rate, and I believe what I charged was somewhat less than other monitors. Incredibly, towards the end of my monitoring career, I was asked to re-submit an invoice because we had charged less than five hundred pounds per day, which had become the standard rate. Another bizarre occurrence was when my invoice included an hour for "thinking" it was challenged on the basis that "we do not pay for thinking".

A question that constantly plagued me was the issue of whether monitoring offered value for money to the taxpayer. I calculated that my monitoring added typically less than 2.6% to a project's grants.

Most project team members told me in the debrief at their end that preparing for my regular inquisition focused their minds and kept them on track. Also, my general project experience was often of significant assistance whilst I acted as a buffer between them and some of the bureaucratic idiosyncrasies of the sponsors. Furthermore, I was able to put them in touch with other relevant researchers in the same field because of my contacts with the sponsors or generally.

The other occasional benefit to a project of them having a monitoring officer was that should disputes arise between the partners, he or she could arbitrate. One common source of such disputes was the divide between academia and business and each side's preconceptions about the other. The academics often had a view that those in commerce and industry were significantly better paid than themselves and their expense entitlements considerably more generous.

Conversely, those in commerce and industry considered academics were, by and large, less pressured and always swanning off to conferences in exotic locations. Where there was serious cause for concern was when academics claimed sole intellectual property rights to the outcomes from the projects in the belief they were the sole intellectual contributors. This, of course, was not necessarily true, and the academics often ignored the fact that their totally grant-funded contribution was risk-free, whereas the business contribution carried significant commercial risk. Also, without the real life experience and data input from the commercial partners, the research could be just pie in the sky.

Repeat business is, of course, the ultimate accolade that one is doing something right, but insofar as my monitoring work goes, there were others. I, along with several others designated by the DTI as "Alpha" monitoring officers, attended a workshop at a conference centre in Abingdon, Oxfordshire, on collaborative research organised by DTI and the Engineering and Physical Sciences Research Council (EPSRC).

The monitoring officers were understandably excluded from a session in which their performance was discussed. However, the paperwork for that session was not omitted from the general conference pack, and I was naturally delighted to see from it that I was the highest marked monitoring officer.

A further indication of how my monitoring was regarded was that I was invited by the DTI to be the main speaker addressing newly appointed monitoring officers on their one-day induction course. Also, one of my monitoring officer reports was used as an example of good practice to other monitoring officers.

All this probably explains why I was invited to a Royal Garden party at Buckingham Palace. Interestingly, Rosemary was included as Mrs Price, so one wonders about the security arrangements.

We celebrated with dinner at the Savoy the night before the garden party and followed up with a reunion with my old CAA team at West Drayton.

Off to the Palace

As with most of my work experience, I gave significant thought to the purpose of monitoring and how it should be conducted, and my conclusions I recorded in a series of unsolicited documents. These were targeted at projects teams so that they could easily assimilate what was required of them in the monitoring process, as well as the monitoring officers themselves. Perhaps naively, I put these into the public domain without seeking any remuneration for myself.

Another initiative I undertook was to have the DTI administrative staff invited singly as observers to a project progress meeting. Otherwise, they had a limited notion of what occurred and hence seeing monitoring in "action" helped them understand more fully the whole process. Incidentally, it also improved the liaison between them and the monitoring officers.

Given all the above, it was, therefore, with a combination of annoyance and amusement that I was told around 2005 that if I wanted to have any further monitoring work, I would have to go on a training course for monitoring officers. Although those making the request admitted it was ludicrous, they were adamant I had to attend if I wanted any further work. The matter appeared even more bizarre when upon examining the briefing material for monitoring officers that I was sent, I noticed a significant amount of the content was identical to the documents that I had produced for free and put into the public domain. There was no overt acknowledgement of my authorship of the documents; however, on examining the internal properties of electronic copies, my name duly appeared as the author.

Nevertheless, despite much of the wording in these documents being mine, there were certain additions and alterations that introduced concepts that I considered nonsensical, and I therefore requested that my name be removed from the documents as I felt they impugned my credibility. I cannot be sure, but I have a strong suspicion that these amended versions of my documents were produced by external consultants to the DTI who had charged for them.

I soon had a further indication of the new order when, at an event for projects, including some that I was already monitoring, I was shyly approached by an external consultant to the DTI who informed me he was now my monitoring liaison officer, and all communication to the DTI and research councils should be routed through him. When I questioned his credentials for undertaking such a role, it immediately became apparent he had very little practical experience of monitoring.

Perhaps it was partly my own fault that such a situation had arisen because for some time, I had been so immersed in my other activities, including coordinating a research programme (see Chapter 21), that I had failed to keep my ear to the ground on developments at the DTI. These included that there had been a policy change, and instead of the DTI sponsoring research programmes on specific projects, there would be an all-embracing programme called the Technology Programme.

Apart from my qualms about its internal processes and the naiveté of the external consultants assisting in setting it up, the title disturbed me. Along with many others, I considered we had technology coming out of our ears, and what was required was a programme addressing societal and commercial objectives that technology may or may not be required to support. Indeed when a continuation of the Alvey Programme was being mooted, I had suggested that rather than continuing to pursue further technology, it should address the exploitation of what technology we had included in its sales and marketing, particularly as this was something in which the UK was weak.

I found all this extremely frustrating, and as I was approaching retirement, Rosemary and others considered it would be best if I gave up monitoring. Nevertheless, I gave it one last shot and sought and got a contract to monitor five projects in a programme that also involved the Department of Transport and was concerned with road charging and related issues.

By now, the DTI was no more, and the Technology Programme was run by a start-up quango called the Technology Strategy Board (TSB). My monitoring of these last five projects confirmed to me that the overly bureaucratic approach to monitoring that the DTI had embarked on was made worse by the setting up of the TSB. Issues that could be settled by a phone call to the relevant DTI official when I first started monitoring now involved a convoluted chain involving the MLO and/or the National Engineering Laboratory (NEL). The NEL's involvement was that they had been commissioned to run the administrative side of the Technology Programme and that they did this using an inflexible, unresponsive, and unreliable IT system did not help. Apart from reducing the effectiveness of monitoring, this also meant extra, unnecessary expenditure of my time, taking more than the two days per quarter for which I was being paid.

The final straw was when one of the industrial partners in one of the five projects submitted a claim for a period of time long after the academic partner had finished working on the project. Therefore it had finished as a collaborative research project - collaboration being a pre-requisite of the grant.

Furthermore, I had had my last meeting with the project team sometime before, and the industrial partner was aware of that at the time. I therefore refused to accept the claim, but the company went direct to the TSB, who then amazingly expected me to sign off the claim. Given that the claim broke all the rules and that, in any case, I was not in a position to confirm or otherwise that the work that justified the claim had been done, I refused.

Nevertheless, the TSB went ahead and paid the claim. As a taxpayer, I was appalled, and for me, the whole episode called into question the entire concept of monitoring, I therefore decided that I would cease monitoring for the TSB immediately.

Although I was by then retired, I was still in touch with members of the collaborative research community, including monitoring officers, and learnt with dismay that the TSB had become even more hidebound and unnecessarily bureaucratic. I, therefore, in 2010, wrote to David Willetts, who, as the Minister for Universities and Science, was responsible for the TSB, to express my concerns. He personally replied, and a meeting was arranged between myself and the then TSB's Director of Operations and Services.

It turned out he was a short-term secondee from one of the large consultancies, which may have partly explained the problem. I thought there was some meeting of minds and was assured my observations would be taken into account in a review TSB was having into its processes. However, some five years on, the TSB appears to be even more entrenched in its unrealism. This includes monitoring officers being expected to perform their monitoring in one and a half days per quarter. My belief is that this is insufficient for a monitoring officer to execute the necessary diligence, and monitoring is now, therefore, pointless and a waste of money.

The Technology Strategy Board did, however, later make one sensible decision in re-branding itself as Innovate UK, thus meeting my objection to the technology focus and titling referred to previously.

Although I had given up monitoring for the TSB, I did one more monitoring assignment before I retired. Professor Peter Brandon, pro vice-chancellor for research at Salford University, having seen me in action monitoring one of his projects, asked if I would like to monitor a project in which his future daughter-in-law was involved. This was a collaboration between the charity arm of Warrington Wolves Rugby League Club and Thorn Cross Young Offenders Institute. The project's aim was the rehabilitation of young offenders by involving them in sport. Thus with this non-technology topic, I ended a part of my career that had involved me in a considerable number of often fascinating areas.

Stan Price

CHAPTER 20

PROJECTS MONITORED

As indicated, my monitoring work luckily saw me involved in a fascinating variety of sectors, technologies and situations. The second project I monitored was one of these, albeit in a negative way. It involved a consortium, which included International Computers Ltd (ICL) and the National Computing Centre (NCC). Its objective was to define a comprehensive set of metrics to cover the whole of the software development process and then set up a database of values for these metrics culled from actual projects.

Initially, I was very impressed by the way the project went about its business. The timing and quality of its progress meetings, reports and general conduct were impeccable. Indeed, the theoretical work defining the metrics was successfully carried out. However, the smooth process disguised the fact that the population of the database was in trouble, and the project ended with very little data having been collected.

The lesson to be learnt from the project was that a good project administration does not necessarily deliver a good project outcome. Indeed, several projects I monitored had appalling administration and yet published excellent research results. These included some involving Cambridge University, where the academics involved gave the impression that administration was beneath them, but they could not be overly censured over this because of the impressive end products.

Arguably, the most successful of all the projects I monitored was one early in my monitoring career. The consortium undertaking it consisted of GEC Semiconductors, Reading University and a small software house. Its objective was to produce a real time scheduling system for a wafer fabrication plant. The majority of wafer fabrication plants produce small batches of circuit boards, with each batch following a different path between various stages, involving expensive equipment and highly qualified staff. To maximise the product yield from such a plant was critical, particularly given the relative unreliability of the equipment scheduling, hence the purpose of the Project.

The resultant product was so successful that Intel adopted it for all their plants worldwide. Unfortunately, this meant that meeting Intel's needs would have constituted too high a proportion of the total business of the software house's which was responsible for the exploitation of the product. This was unacceptable to Intel, so to secure the order and provide security for its staff, the software house had to sell out to a larger US company. Incidentally, the owner of the software house received several million pounds as a result of the sale.

I believed this Project was such an outstanding example of what could be achieved by government assistance that the story of the Project should have been documented as a case study. I therefore suggested this to the DTI; however, they were uninterested in pursuing it. I also believed that the scheduling scenario for the wafer fabrication plant was potentially similar to that for a hospital with patients substituting for circuit board batches. A letter to the National Health Services (NHS's) chief scientist suggesting this, unfortunately, produced a response that only could only come under the heading of, Uninterested As Not Invented Here.

The history of the project was also interesting in two respects:

- GEC's involvement resulted from their takeover of Plessey Semiconductors. Initially, when Plessey were involved, the intention was to develop the system using the experimental wafer fabrication plant at Plessey's Caswell Laboratory. However, on taking over, Plessey GEC closed the Caswell Laboratory. Development of the Project was transferred to the actual wafer fabrication production plant at Roborough near Plymouth. Whether this contributed to the success of the project is a moot point.

- After two years of development, it was becoming apparent that the approach being taken was a dead end. However, a more elegant, generic approach had been identified during the course of this development. The experienced project manager therefore did not hesitate but took the decision to junk what had been produced so far and go with the generic approach. This latter approach was so elegant that the amount of software that had to be developed and tested was much reduced, and this meant the overall timescale of the project was only marginally extended. The lesson to be drawn was the criticality to project success of fearless, decisive project management.

This project was also characterised by the deliberate attempt of the project management to socially bind the personnel from the three consortium members by, for example, having a project dinner the night before every quarterly meeting. This was held, on most occasions, in an excellent bistro in the old Barbican area of Plymouth. Rosemary came with me to Plymouth and attended one dinner, but this was a rare event. The only other times she travelled with me was when the project meeting venue fitted in with something she wanted to do. For example, she accompanied me on my trips to York so that she could meet up with her half-sister who travelled down from Northallerton. I should add the cost of her accompanying me came out of our own pockets and not PPSL and certainly not the clients.

As I have indicated previously, I personally put great stress on the importance of such measures to increase the social integration of the members of a team for improving the chances of the team achieving its objectives. Unfortunately, there are some who, through naivety or political malice, criticise such measures, particularly where taxpayer's money is involved, and of course, care should be taken to ensure the expenditure involved is not excessive.

I ran into such criticism with a project, which decided to have a three-day workshop at Brampton near Carlisle. I suggested as a team-building exercise that the project should replace an afternoon session with an evening one, and on the resultant spare afternoon, I would take the team on a short hike along the nearby Hadrian's Wall. To this end, I sent a message to all workshop participants to bring suitable clothing and footwear.

The message was seen by the senior management of one of the participating organisations who objected in the strongest manner to their personnel going on a "jolly". I retorted by pointing out the benefits to be obtained by such an exercise and that those involved would be working hours in the evening to compensate.

My arguments were accepted, and the hike went ahead with everyone participating. This included a very glamorous lady member of the project team who had not brought the appropriate gear yet gamely came along. The sight of her in a vivid scarlet coat and stiletto heels following the paths that the Roman Legionnaires had trod is an enduring memory.

Many other projects recognised the importance of such social activities in team building. One in particular combined social activities with the vital but often neglected involvement of the final end users of the technology being developed. It also had workshops in a convivial peaceful location.

The project involved the development of expert systems to support the design and costing of building projects. It was led by the University of Salford, with the representative users being provided by the Royal Institute of Chartered Surveyors (RICS). The venue for these workshops was the rather upmarket Armathwaite Hall at the northern end of Bassenthwaite Lake in the English Lake District. However, here I must confess that whilst the Project members were hard at work, the DTI/Research Council representative and I took off along some of the lakeside walks with which I had become familiar on previous visits to the area.

Another project, which combined attention to the social requirements with workshops and meetings in scenic locations, was one with a consortium that had several member organisations from Northern Ireland. One of its meetings at the academic prime partner, Queens College, Belfast, was followed by an excellent seafood dinner in a pub on the shores of Strangford Lough.

This was where I was introduced to Chilean wines for the first time. Perhaps wrongly, I had been identified as the leading bon vivant in the assembled company and, as such, was asked to choose the wines. I chose an Australian Chardonnay. I was then approached by the wine waiter who suggested the Chilean Chardonnay instead, which was somewhat cheaper but turned out much superior to the Australian I was expecting. This project also hosted one of the most memorable workshops.

This was at an inn by a cove on the Antrim coast adjacent to the Giants Causeway, which was visited along with the nearby Bushmills Distillery. I was awakened one morning, whilst staying at the inn, by shouting outside and, upon looking out of the bedroom window, saw several project members pushing the principal researcher's Jaguar car along the very misty coast road past the inn.

Apparently, the damp mist had come off the sea by way of the offshore Rathlin Island and had got into the car's electrics, and it was unable to start. My shouted comments that they were unlikely to succeed in starting it because they were impractical academics did not go down well.

The project was also interesting in that one of the Northern Ireland industrial partners was the aviation company, Short Brothers. They hosted a couple of meetings in a conference room on the site where the Titanic had been built. Shorts having taken over the site from the builders of the Titanic, Harland and Wolff. Despite this omen, the project was relatively successful.

I also monitored another project, which, on one occasion, was far from a pleasant experience. All members of the consortium were Northern Ireland based, although this had nothing to do with the unpleasantness. The DTI lost their files relating to the project, and to compound the problem, they did not recognise their loss and assumed that as they had no information, the project was performing poorly. They therefore wrote to the project expressing their concerns without, incredibly, informing me.

As soon as I walked into the next quarterly meeting at the University of Ulster, I was aware that there was an atmosphere. The lead researcher, a formidable lady professor, instantly laid into me, accusing me of being two-faced in expressing my satisfaction with the project to them, whilst reporting back negatively to the sponsors.

However, I had always adopted a policy of telling a project what I was saying about them, and fortunately, I was able to convince this project that I was not guilty. Happily, after some coordination with the DTI, the situation was resolved.

While integrated team working in a project consortium contributed greatly to the success of a project even though individuals were employed by different organisations, clearly the level of expertise, experience and commitment of the individuals themselves was also a vital factor.

However, one had to be careful of judging this on the basis of invalid stereotypes. I was very concerned when the manager of one project, who was also the conceiver of the project, left his company, and hence the project. Adding to my concern was the fact that his replacement was a relatively elderly lady with a motherly disposition. But I need not have worried; her social skills carried the Project forward successfully and arguably were more suited to the implementation phase than those of the original conceivers. Also, I deduced she represented less of a competitive threat to the young Turks that composed most of the staff of the project, thus ensuring their cooperation.

Not all project managers were of the necessary calibre. One was so inexperienced and tentative in the role that I took the time out to give him some individual coaching. This included stopping off at Milton Keynes, where he was based, and meeting up with him in the station buffet as I travelled between Manchester and London.

Actually, my efforts were in vain because the lead partner, for whom he worked, folded before the end of the project. This was very unfortunate because the aim of the project was most innovative and involved the reduction of leakage in water networks by reducing pressure hotspots. It did this by a computer system controlling the flow using valves located at key junctions in a network. The amount of water saved by such a system which cost hundreds of thousands of pounds was apparently the same as what would have been saved by leak proofing a water network or building new dams and reservoirs, both solutions costing millions of pounds.

Although not a project manager, a lead member of a project came to an ignominious end by being sent to prison. This was not because of his involvement with the project but with a related project. Both involved the computer scanning of the human body to facilitate better fitting clothes. The other project was specialising in gravity suits for Royal Air Force pilots. The individual concerned persuaded those participants being scanned that there was a need for the gravity suits to cope with the wearer having an erection whilst wearing them. He therefore masturbated them prior to scanning. Unfortunately for him, one of his models was underage, hence the conviction.

The project I was monitoring was scanning 10,000 male and female members of the general public as part of a national survey in order to come up with a more accurate and updated set of clothing sizes. Clearly, this Project would be compromised if the odium from the other Project transferred across, but despite the conviction hitting the UK national press, this was avoided, and the survey was a success.

Indeed one of the additional outcomes was that the leading partners of the UK project became consultants to other national human sizing surveys worldwide.

The overall project, as well as the sizing survey, included research into the measurements necessary to define a humans shape and how, if you had your shape held digitally, you could see how you looked in clothes being retailed via the internet.

It was one of the largest, if not the largest, of all the projects I monitored and involved nearly all the major UK clothing retailers and academic partners, including University College London and the London College of Fashion, plus a Japanese scanner manufacturer. I should add the imprisoned individual was not employed by any of these but by another partner.

As well as the individuals working on a project acting harmoniously, it was also important that the consortium members at the organisational level cooperated together. Sometimes, although the individuals got on well together, their organisations did not, and vice versa. With a couple of projects, this was sometimes so bad that litigation was contemplated, although, in the end, the disagreements did not reach that stage. On these occasions, my monitoring role became partly a mediating role.

Inevitably, sometimes organisations within projects had to drop out. Invariably, these were commercial partners, with market and financial factors being largely the reasons behind their withdrawal. Although the withdrawing consortium members were supposed to find a replacement, on one occasion, the two commercial partners withdrew without finding replacements leaving only the academic partner as the sole participant in the project.

On another occasion, a partner withdrew but made alternative reparations under pressure from another partner who happened to be a major client. The former was the Digital Equipment Corporation (DEC), and the latter the NatWest Bank. The reparations consisted of DEC donating a number of upmarket desktop and laptop computers to the remaining consortium members. The project also included a desktop for PPSL. And not only that, another consortium member, Lancaster University, set it up for me, including my original connection to the Internet and E-Mail. Upon reflection, this clearly compromised my impartiality in monitoring the project, but the DTI, when I reported it to them, did not seem to mind.

The subject matter and outcome of this project were also of interest. The NatWest Bank, like many other UK banks, had taken functions that were common to all branches out of the branches and centralised them. Not surprisingly, this introduced communications problems between these centralised functions and a less than seamless service to the bank customers.

Naively, the senior management of NatWest felt some form of information technology could rectify the situation, and the purpose of the project was to do just that. Not surprisingly, the project concluded that a more sensible solution was regular get-to-know each other sessions between the branch and centralised staff, with the only information technology component being a few E-Mail templates.

Although monitoring officers intervention in projects was discouraged generally, so they could retain and be seen to retain their objectivity, on some rare occasions, I did intervene when I felt the project and its objectives were in jeopardy. One such was when one of the project partners decided to make two key members of the project team redundant. To do this, it was necessary for the company concerned to show the work being undertaken by the two individuals was no longer required. However, I pointed out that the company had an agreement with the DTI to perform the project work. As a result of my intervention, the threat of redundancy was withdrawn, and the project was saved.

Many other projects were straightforward to monitor, and this allowed me to take more of an interest in their subject matter. They included:

- Development of a computer system to control the environment of greenhouses, particularly in the event of sensor failure. This involved the Silsoe Horticultural Centre near Bedford.
- Remote control over the internet of the environmental and domestic functions in different types of building and building up a database of usage statistics.
- Using artificial intelligence techniques to schedule the usage of University lecture halls.

- Increasing the reliability of a blood-testing machine, which processed several thousand samples per hour.

A full list of the projects I monitored, with principal details, can be found in Appendix 1.

The final tranche of five projects I monitored had a local Manchester connection. The Department of Transport had unwisely assumed the residents of Greater Manchester would vote for a road traffic congestion-charging scheme. They had, therefore, in conjunction with the TSB, set up a number of projects, including the five, to investigate road charging.

Unfortunately, the sensible citizens of Greater Manchester voted five to one against the scheme. Therefore, it was interesting to watch the projects cosmetically refocus themselves to fit in with the new Realpolitik.

Stan Price

CHAPTER 21

RESEARCH PROGRAMME COORDINATOR

As mentioned previously, the projects I monitored were themselves part of programmes devoted to particular topics. Generally, each programme had a coordinator who, as the name suggests, was tasked with facilitating the interaction between the projects in the particular programme. This had a number of objectives, including avoiding any duplication of effort, but with the overall objective of making the outcomes of the programme greater than the sum of the individual project's outcomes.

One programme was devoted to safety critical systems, i.e. systems concerned with preventing death and/or injury or those which, if they failed, could cause death and/or injury. There was also a covert purpose of the programme: the improvement of the software development process generally. The safety aspect, although legitimate, was included in order to increase the prospect of its being funded. The programme comprised some thirty-two projects, three of which I monitored. Partway through the course of the programme, the coordinator, Bob Malcolm, took up a European posting in Bilbao. Given my interest and experience in both the overt safety critical objective and the covert systems development objective, I threw my cap in the ring to succeed him. No one was appointed to replace Bob;

nevertheless, I was to become heavily involved in a coordination role aided by several others.

My involvement resulted in two specific initiatives, both of which I conceived and got approval and funding for. The first of these was a series of seven workshops devoted to specific topics which I considered were of key relevance to successful and particularly safe systems. My judgement on what was key was heavily influenced by my previous industrial experience. To make the workshops manageable, the number attending was restricted to twenty or less, split equally between academia and industry, largely but not exclusively, drawn from participants in the safety critical programme that I rated.

I chaired the workshops, and each had a rapporteur who produced a report chronicling the proceedings and the conclusions. This was circulated to the attendees for their comments, and a final version incorporating these was then published. The workshops were opened by myself with an introduction that cited the purpose of the workshop and its format.

The latter, after the introduction, consisted of presentations from the safety critical programme projects that were relevant to the topic of the workshop. These were followed by comments on the presentations from the catalysts, which led into general discussions followed by a summary.

The initial workshop, under the title, 'What goes on out there?' addressed the gulf between what the research community thought happened in day-to-day industrial/commercial practice and what actually happened. As well as the DTI sponsorship of the workshop, it also was run under the auspices of the Safety Critical Systems Club. This was run by the Centre for Software Reliability at Newcastle University, and over the years, I made contributions to several of its events.

The other workshops that followed the initial one addressed the following, in relation to the safety of systems:

- Human Factors
- Software Requirements Elicitation and Capture
- System Assessment
- Artificial Intelligence
- Process Models
- Data

These later workshops, unlike the first, which lasted one day and was held in a DTI building in Central London, were held in Country Hotels over two days which allowed time for informal discussions and networking. This also allowed me to introduce my trademark feature, an afternoon walk.

The Isaak Walton Hotel in the Peak Districts' Dovedale was used on more than one occasion, and the walk there took in tea at Ayrs Cottage on the bluffs overlooking the Dale. This came as a surprise to many workshop attendees as approaching Ayrs Cottage. With its unprepossessing appearance, there was no sign that it offered refreshments.

Another Derbyshire venue for one of the Workshops was the Moorside Hotel south of Stockport. Here the afternoon walk took in Lyme Park, which was later to be the setting for the BBC`s production of Jane Austen's Pride and Prejudice. Unfortunately, the walk was rather late in the afternoon for the time of year, and the party found itself locked in the park. Fortunately, a high decrepit style was discovered, over which we made our escape before the light was lost.

Given that they were my idea, I cannot be objective about the usefulness of these workshops. However, nearly all the attendees felt they advanced their thinking on the various topics, and as they were of significant status and not the types to indulge in platitudes, I am inclined to a positive view on my endeavours.

This cannot be said of my second initiative under the auspices of the safety critical systems programme. This was based on my conviction that if one wanted to propagate good practice, and particularly when guidance was required at the relevant time and place, brevity was of the essence. I therefore suggested a series of leaflets promoting safety, none of which was to be more than two pages, with each one dedicated to a particular aspect of systems delivery and operation.

The DTI agreed to pay for their production, and so I put together a small team, which included Bob Malcolm, who by then had returned from Bilbao, to draft them.

The plan was for them then to be subjected to both general and peer review before they were disseminated. The reviewers include personnel from the UK Health and Safety Executive (HSE), which had appeared to give its consent to the whole initiative. It was therefore surprising that just prior to the first of the leaflets being sent out, the HSE advised the DTI not to proceed any further. Given the HSE's prime public sector responsibilities for safety matters, the DTI was forced to draw the plug on the initiative. I was not aware of any reason for their about-turn, other than the HSE protecting its patch, but it saddened me that something that could have improved general safety was stopped after taxpayer's money had been spent for no purpose.

Soon after the end of the Safety Critical Systems Programme, an opportunity arose to once more take over from Bob Malcolm in coordinating a collaborative research programme. This was in response to an invitation to tender from the Engineering and Physical Sciences Research Council (EPSRC). What was puzzling was that

Bob was not only performing the role but wished to continue to do so and had also responded to the invitation to tender.

In the event, Bob was justifiably chosen. The interesting aspect of the process was that I perceived that my lack of an academic grounding in the topic of the programme would count against me. I therefore mugged up for the interview by reading a large number of academic papers in the domain, but to no avail, because none of the questions in the interview were related to the academic content of the programme.

Nevertheless, it was not long before I got a further opportunity for coordinating a research programme. I received an invitation to tender from the DTI for monitoring work on a new collaborative research programme but unusually combined with it was the opportunity to tender for the coordinator's job. So I naturally tendered for both and was invited to an interview for the coordinator role. The interview panel consisted of DTI and EPSRC personnel, and I was, of course, pleased that they offered me the job, an offer that I naturally accepted.

The title of the programme was the Management of Information, which was a total misnomer, possibly for some political reason of which I never became aware. What the programme really addressed was fraud, privacy and security. The programme had a budget of just over fifteen million pounds and resulted in sixteen projects, with their grant awards being spread over three tranches between March 1999 and October 2000. The programme had an advisory panel, on which I sat, and a pool of six monitoring officers who monitored the sixteen projects between them.

Initially, my role was to be involved in the solicitation of proposals for projects and assistance to those making these proposals. A couple of the proposals came about at my suggestion. Fifty-four outline proposals were eventually forthcoming, and these were whittled down via a full proposal stage to the sixteen proposals that were eventually selected. The Advisory Panel was responsible for making the selections, and every consortium to which a grant offer was made both accepted their grant and participated in the programme.

Given that all six monitoring officers were experienced, I did not unduly interfere in their monitoring of the projects, nor indeed in how the projects were executed, except on the rare occasions when there were major problems. One of these was a breakdown in the relationship between the project and its monitoring officer, where I had to replace the monitoring officer with another from the pool.

I did, however, provide the monitoring officers with the documents I had produced on monitoring. Also, I attended one quarterly meeting of each project each year. This was generally in order for me to assess face-to-face how they were getting on, thus supplementing the information I gleaned from the project and monitoring officer reports.

Most of my effort as programme coordinator went on ensuring that the results of the programme were greater than the sum of the results of the individual projects. This, of course, included making sure that there was no duplication of effort, although, in the event, there was little occurrence of this.

My approach to achieving this aim was firstly to identify clusters of common interest or purpose between the projects, with a wide input from others, and which were:

- Authentication, both artefacts and people
- Biometrics, particularly facial recognition
- Closed Circuit Television
- Abnormality detection
- Trust
- Technology Deployment

There were naturally some projects that contributed to more than one cluster.

Within, the clusters I was proactive in ensuring there were the maximum awareness and dialogue, if not cooperation between the projects in a cluster. One of the principal ways I did this was by having a stream in the programme workshops for each cluster and even encouraging the project members to give joint presentations.

I organised six workshops during the course of the programme. Apart from the initial one-day workshop, they were all spread over two days to allow a social evening for the essential informal networking. In essence, as well as the clustering objective, the aims of the workshops were:

- For projects to cross-brief each other.
- For projects to brief a wider audience, which was invited, about themselves and the programme. This particularly applied to the last three workshops, where the projects had some results to show.
- To brief the members of the programme community on wider research and research opportunities. To this end, some of the workshops were briefed by the relevant official from the European Commission.
- Address the tensions between privacy and security. One notable success of this was a debate at the second workshop between the invited head of Privacy International and a leading academic technologist.

In organising and running these workshops, the monitoring officers and my partner, Rosemary, who worked for PPSL, assisted me. I believe the workshops were generally successful. For example, the fourth workshop held at the then University of Manchester Institute of Science and Technology Conference Centre had 155 attendees, of whom 90 were involved in the programme, and the remaining 65 were guests.

Pontificating at an MI Workshop.

In addition to the workshops, cross-fertilisation between the projects was facilitated by a monthly newsletter and a website. The former I produced and distributed electronically, but the latter was managed by a technology transfer coordinator, although I made a significant input to the content.

Unfortunately, at one stage, the website was hacked, which was most embarrassing given the security remit of the programme. This was not the only occasion the technology transfer coordination function caused me grief. The split coordination function was a usual feature of the programme, contrasting with all of the other programmes with which I participated, having only one coordinator whose role included both the research and technology transfer aspects.

Generally, I believed the separate coordination situation was not workable, but particularly so in the case of the Management of Information Programme because the chosen technology company was essentially only a public relations agency. They did not understand my position, that after the initial need to advertise the Programme in order to garner participation, there was little need for publicity until the projects and the programme started producing results.

Despite my explaining this to them, in the interim period, they were constantly pestering for unnecessary publicity material, which, apart from trying my patience, meant that when it came to the end of the programme, and there were results to publicise, they had an insufficient budget to do so. To be fair to them, it may well be they were under pressure to advertise the fact that the DTI, and government in general, were doing something rather than just ensuring that the taxpayers" money was not being wasted.

The only other significant problem I encountered in coordinating the programme was that the Home Office's and Ministry of Defence's initial interest in the programme was not sustained, and more specifically, no funding was forthcoming from them. I attempted to rekindle the waning interest of particularly the Home Office by briefing them on progress. This produced the amusing scenario of Home Office departments becoming aware of other Home Office departments, which until I brought them together, they did not know existed.

Generally, with a few exceptions, the usefulness of research programmes like the Management of Information, particularly in terms of a commercial return, could not be judged until some time, including years, after they ended. Normally and surprisingly, little significant effort was made by the sponsoring government departments to judge this. One would have thought this would have been essential in order to discover whether the investment of taxpayer's money in such programmes was justified.

However, sometime after the programme had finished, along with my involvement, I was asked by the relevant research council, EPSRC, to investigate the outcomes of the individual projects. Although there was no question of my being paid, given my own natural curiosity, I undertook a brief study. Most gratifyingly, this revealed that all but two of the sixteen projects had produced a marketable product or at least a demonstrator. These were not the only useful outcomes. The projects had also been useful in influencing standards, academic courses and future research.

One particularly pleasing outcome was that because of my influence, two leading academics working in the same field, which had hitherto been at loggerheads, jointly published a book.

I have no reason to believe that other similar collaborative research programmes did not have similar outcomes and that, therefore, all my efforts monitoring and coordinating over twenty or so years were of some use.

CHAPTER 22

EXPERT WITNESS

I was giving a talk at a conference when, as a joke, I asked my audience, "What is the last stage in the software life cycle?"

The answer I supplied was litigation, and on the flight home, this set me thinking. Associated in my mind with the law and lawyers was money. These thoughts were against a background of the UK having just passed the Consumer Protection Act and the usual stories of computer cock-ups and failed IT projects appearing in the media.

It seemed the way for me to pursue this thought was to become an expert witness in IT, to which end I believed I was qualified, and so I started to research the possibilities.

It appeared that to become really credible as an IT expert witness, one had to get on the British Computer Society (BCS) Expert Witness Panel. As I was already a member, this seemed the way forward. However, to become elected to the panel, you had effectively to be apprenticed for a time to an existing panel member who would mentor you. There were at the time only eight individuals on the panel, which in itself indicated to me that this was indeed worth pursuing, and I therefore approached one of the panel members, Professor Sandy Douglas, with a view to his mentoring me.

Sandy was a retired academic from the London School of Economics who functioned as an expert witness through a company called Buxton Douglas Ltd. Professor John Buxton was in many ways the Godfather of Software Engineering. He had co-authored the proceedings of the 1968 NATO conference that created the concept of Software Engineering and was an adviser to the Pentagon on the creation of the ADA real time language under the Stoneman Project. He had also set up the highly regarded Software Engineering Department at Warwick University and then the one at my old college, Kings London. At the time, his other involvements precluded him from undertaking much expert witness work, but he was a director of Buxton Douglas.

I had formed an acquaintanceship with John through the DTI work, despite my giving a negative review to a book he had written. Therefore asking Sandy Douglas to mentor me was pushing against an open door, and in parallel, I joined Buxton Douglas as a partner. As well as Sandy, three of the other partners were on the BCS expert witness panel, so I was soon a member of the IT expert witness in-crowd.

Buxton Douglas was based in Temple Chambers adjacent to the Inner Temple, and my involvement meant monthly trips to London to review each other's cases and the progress of the company. Initially, I also attended to Southwark Crown Court to observe, as part of my expert witness apprenticeship, a case in which Sandy Douglas was acting as an expert witness.

This involved a young man who was accused of causing criminal damage by hacking into several university computer systems around the UK. He was charged with criminal damage because the later computer misuse act, which covered hacking, was not yet on the statute book.

At first, I thought how could he have caused criminal damage, because superficially, he was not doing anything physical. However, it was pointed out to me that what he had done did indeed impact the physical state of the hacked computers hard drives by changing the electrons on their surface.

Another interesting aspect of the case was that the accused worked from his bedroom in Essex, and one of the universities he had hacked into was Strathclyde in Scotland. There was, therefore, some discussion in court as to whether the charges pertaining to Strathclyde should be tried under English or Scottish law. The judge finally pragmatically resolved this, pointing out there was a significant number of charges relating to English Universities, and it would not sufficiently alter the case if the Scottish dimension was dropped.

Before joining Buxton Douglas and just after, I was involved with a number of fitness for purpose cases. The outcomes varied between the courts finding for the IT supplier and the courts finding for the IT customer, dependant on the contract: written or assumed. Apart from the legal side, these cases threw some light on my thinking on the difficulties of specifying IT systems. However, I was soon to be involved in a criminal case that was much more interesting.

I acted for the defendant, who was a payroll clerk with British Rail in Carlisle. She was charged on four counts that she had altered information on the payroll computer system so that she was paid more than she was entitled to. Amazingly, although the total amount was only approximately £250, the trial went on for two weeks with the cost of a judge, senior and junior barristers for the Crown and the defendant, myself and the court staff running into tens of thousands of pounds.

We were into the second week of the trial when, cross-examining the British Rail managers appearing for the prosecution, the defence counsel, prompted by me, got these witnesses to admit that there was an equally innocent explanation as opposed to a malfeasant one with respect to one of the charges. The charge related to her claiming for work on a rest day rather than a normal workday, which could have been caused by her accidentally pressing an adjacent key on a keyboard instead of the intended one.

The judge, therefore, directed that this charge be thrown out, leaving just three. As well as the charge itself being dismissed the number of charges hence incidents was important. The prosecution had claimed that only two similar incidents involving two other employees records out of a thousand had been discovered in a six month period, whereas four had been found in the defendant's records over a two year period. I was surprised at this bogus use of statistics, but this was before several high profile cases involving the misuse of statistics hit the headlines. However, there were still three charges for the defendant to face, but these were soon dismissed, albeit on a technicality.

The defendant worked on a local IBM minicomputer at Carlisle, networked to the main British Rail payroll ICL computer system in Nottingham, where the payroll slips were printed out. The Police and Criminal Evidence (PACE) rules required that a certificate signed by a responsible person, confirming that the computer was working satisfactorily at the time, should accompany any computer-produced evidence.

Late into the second week of the trial, it was realised that the certificates appertaining to the payroll slips referred to the IBM minicomputer rather than to the ICL computer, which they should have done. The payroll slips were therefore ruled inadmissible as evidence, and without this evidence of what she had been paid, the prosecution case with respect to the three charges collapsed, and the judge directed the jury to find the defendant not guilty.

I myself felt a little guilty as maybe I should have spotted the IBM/ICL confusion earlier, and then I would have forgone several days fees. Also, it would have meant only two or three days instead of ten staying at a Country House Hotel where the chef had come from the Dorchester.

Civil cases could also be interesting. The founder and managing director of a company that sold fast food accessories to the catering trade was on holiday when he got a phone call that something funny was going on with his company. He immediately returned to find the company's premises deserted and his co-directors and workers operating an identical company up the road serving his client base.

Naturally, he sued the new company, and part of his case was that they had copied data from his company's computer to that of the new company. His solicitor instructed me to investigate whether this could be proved. Using a legal device called an Anton Piller order, I obtained copies of the new company's computer files and compared them to those of the old company. I concentrated on spelling errors within the data and showed conclusively that spelling errors were consistent between the two systems. For example, instances where "pizza" was spelt "piza" was one hundred percent consistent between the two systems. I could, therefore, confidently say to the court that electronic copying had taken place.

Another case revealed the quirkiness of the law. An accountant who unwisely attempted to advise his client on the procurement of a computer system was held to be responsible when the system that was supplied proved not to be fit for purpose. Although the system was actually supplied by a third party, a computer company, the accountant, in a letter informing his client about the bids he had solicited for the supply of the system, had headed it "quotation" in the singular rather than the plural. Amazingly, based on the absence of the single letter s, the accountant was deemed by the court to have been the supplier and thus was responsible for the damages incurred by his client because of the system's unfitness for purpose.

A further civil case illustrated how a single software fault could have a disastrous impact on an organisation. A company manufacturing upmarket bed linen operated a stock control system. This failed to correctly handle a peculiarity of the way they operated. This peculiarity was that if a client ordered a certain number of items of bed linen and the supplier was able to produce more than the number ordered from the cloth set aside for the manufacture of the order, the extra items were also supplied.

Unfortunately, the stock control system deducted this larger number from the total number of outstanding items that had been ordered from all clients. This had the effect that the company was under prepared for meeting its delivery commitments and, as a result, suffered in terms of delivery times. The company's business was almost exclusively in the mail order catalogue sector, the publishers of which set a number of performance criteria for those companies that were included.

One of these criteria was delivery times, and the company's failure to meet these because of the fault in the stock control caused major damage to their business. They had to close one of their mills in the northwest of England, and the future of their other one in Nottingham and hence the business as a whole was severely threatened. They therefore sued the supplier of the stock control system and appointed me as an expert witness. My input was to deduce what the software fault was and advise that the system software supplier should have allowed for the peculiarity. However, after that, like many expert witness assignments, I was not made aware of the legal outcome.

One case was frightening rather than interesting. I was asked by a barrister to go over to Northern Ireland to view a piece of software and produce an affidavit to say it was an original piece of work, assuming, of course, I was confident it was. The software was for the E-Prom of a poker-playing gaming machine. Apparently, there was only one supplier of such gaming machines in Northern Ireland. This company either leased the machines direct to pubs and clubs or sold them to third parties who then leased them to pubs and clubs. The company regularly updated the software and provided the updates

to the third parties, as well as to its direct clients. It had decided
to stop supplying these updates to the third parties, presumably
so that the functionality of the third-party offerings would get less
attractive to pubs and clubs. They would therefore be more likely to
deal directly with the company hence threatening the livelihood of
the third parties. Two of these had got together and produced their
own software for the gaming machines, and it was this software I was
asked to possibly certify as an original piece of work. This would be
as a pre-emptive measure in case they should be sued for a copyright
violation by the company.

I flew to Belfast Harbour Airport on a very snowy winter day
when many flights did not take off. I was met in Belfast by the
principal of one of the third parties who was driving a top-of-the-
range black Mercedes with black tinted windows, which prevented
anyone outside looking in. It was suggested that we have lunch in
Armagh, and upon using the pub toilets, I was disconcerted to see in
the graffiti above the urinals "Kill all Brits."

Given my Metropolitan Police background, I began to wonder
if this was not an elaborate kidnap attempt, or worse, the Troubles
being at their height. My fears were increased when my host said,
"the programmer is over the border in Dundalk. Do you mind if we
go via the C roads as I do not want to talk to the Security Forces?"

Not being in a position to refuse, I said yes and off we went.

Although the C-roads were covered in snow, the four-wheel-
drive of the Mercedes coped admirably, and we reached the cottage
home of the programmer. After inspecting printouts of the software,
I naturally agreed, with alacrity, that when I got home, I would
indeed write and sign an affidavit. I was much reassured when my
host was happy with this and did not insist on my producing the
affidavit there and then. I was even more reassured when he drove me
back to Belfast Harbour Airport, where, despite the conditions, my

fight back to Manchester took off on time. Prior to this, I had been offered my fee of several hundred pounds in cash. For the record, I said I preferred to send an invoice, and this proved to be no problem.

Initially, in my expert witness career, I did all my work through Buxton Douglas, but with PPSL invoicing Buxton Douglas and they adding a percentage before invoicing the client. Apart from the expert witness work itself, I attempted, with the full agreement of the partners, to turn myself into Buxton Douglas North. To this end, amongst other things, I organised annual receptions for the northern legal community similar to the one that Buxton Douglas held in the Livery Club, which was then just around the corner from Temple Chambers. The northern one was held in the Committee Room of Lancashire Cricket Club at Old Trafford. This obviously could only be done when there was no first-class or international match on, but on one occasion, it was complemented by Ronnie Irani getting a double century for Lancashire in a second eleven match against Kent.

The middle- to long-term prospect was that I would become a partner in Buxton Douglas, though this would have required me to contribute to the equity. Fortunately, having been warned about Sandy Douglas's potential probity, I did not pursue this, which proved to be a sensible course because Buxton Douglas had to go into receivership. The reason was that although the Company had a significant income, more was being spent on wining and dining in the city. Also, one of the partners was using Buxton Douglas to support his own independent expert witness activities. Although the eventual liquidation did not cause me to lose money because of my investing in the equity, I did lose some thirteen thousand pounds worth of fees that were owed to me.

Nevertheless, I continued with expert work in parallel with my other activities and was soon immersed in what turned out to be my most major and lucrative case.

Electronic Data Systems (EDS) was contracted to supply to the Civil Aviation Authority (CAA) a new computer system at Prestwick in Scotland to support the control of air traffic over the North Atlantic. The CAA cancelled the contract after the design milestone, citing non-performance on the part of EDS and EDS took the CAA to court for some forty-two million pounds. Because of my air traffic control and computer background, I was approached directly by EDS's solicitors to be an expert witness for them.

Curiously, this was not so much for my system development expertise; a team of three other experts was handling that, but on the safety issues in the case. EDS`s legal team believed that the CAA might play the safety card. Unfortunately, my other commitments at the time meant I could not really take up the assignment, and at first, I said no. However, the fee I was eventually offered, a four-figure day rate, plus an agreement that I could employ a researcher, made me change my mind.

The researcher I employed was John Smith, who had been the Plessey manager involved in the 9020 Project during my days with the Civil Aviation Authority and who subsequently had produced the safety case for the London Air Traffic Control Centre. Even with John's assistance, I was pushed to cope with the mountain of documentation that the project had generated and the voluminous dialogue between the opposing experts. Naturally, I had to spend a fair amount of time in London at times at very short notice. On one occasion, I had finished my work at Sheffield University and, after having drinks, was at Sheffield Station at about 9.00 pm when I got a message to report to counsel's chambers in Lincoln's Inn by 9.30 am the next morning.

The trial went on for twenty-five days before a settlement was reached outside the court, the terms of which I was never officially informed of. I spent a fair amount of time in the court, and even when I was not required to be present, I had access to a continuous online transcript via the internet.

Insofar as John's and my inputs to the case were concerned, they were significant in two respects. Firstly we smoked out the fact that the first part of four of the CAA's safety procedures amazingly did not exist, and therefore, their criticism of EDD's safety processes in the case was therefore unrealistic, to say the least. Secondly, in my initial report, I had pointed out that there was no common agreement on how safety should be built into software systems, so their criticism of what EDD was doing was not necessarily valid. The CAA retorted that there was agreement and cited numerous standards. To this, I asked the simple question: if there was a common approach, why was there a need for so many standards, which in some areas were even contradictory.

This high profile case apart my diet of expert witness assignments and I settled down to mainly acting for the defence in criminal cases. It soon became apparent that to perform this satisfactorily, particularly given the steep increase in the capacity of hard disc drives. I needed more than the Norton Utilities, which I had used hitherto, to satisfactorily perform the necessary forensic support work. I therefore undertook an evaluation of the four major forensic software tools that were then on the market. I decided that the Forensic Toolkit (FTK) from the Access Data Corporation best suited my requirements, and I spent over one thousand pounds on a licence. My background thoughts were that I could generate a market for Price Project Services sufficient for me to employ people who could take over from me when I reached retirement. The company would therefore have a value, which, if sold on, would augment my pension funds. There was also the possibility of me keeping it in the family, with one common law son-in-law having the necessary technical skills and another the administrative skills.

What FTK enabled me to do was to take a mirror image of a hard drive, DVD, CD, etc, and analyse its contents without impacting the original. This was an important requirement of PACE rules with respect to the handling of computer evidence. Then FTK enabled me to readily view all files, E-Mails, etc, on the media, whether extant or deleted (deleting a file does not, of course, remove it, it just makes the space available for re-use and the file contents etc, remain accessible until they are overwritten, which can be after a long time) and sort them by type, author, creation date and so on.

There was, however, a significant drawback to building a company around computer criminal expert witness work for the defence. It was stressful as not only was it incumbent on one to be absolutely sure of one's facts because your client's reputation and possibly freedom depended on it, but also the attitude of the prosecution and particularly the police was unhelpful. Consistently, the police would have the computer evidence for many months before releasing it to me a few days before the trial, leaving little time for the often-lengthy forensic work to be done. On one occasion, they even refused to release it on the grounds I was not a proper person, and our counsel had to get the judge to order its release to me.

It also became apparent that there was a tendency for the prosecution to exaggerate the magnitude of the alleged crime. One case concerned a computer maintenance technician working for British Nuclear Fuels Ltd (BNFL) at Sellafield in Cumbria. He was provided with inadequate workspace and as he worked close to the Sellafield plant, he used to take computer equipment backwards and forwards between work and home in order to work at home. This was done quite openly with the equipment on the back seat of his car in full view of the British Nuclear constabulary officers manning the Sellafield gates.

Inevitably, in the course of time, he accumulated a stack of broken, redundant or obsolete parts at his home. For some reason, after he had left employment at Sellafield, his home was raided, and this equipment was seized, and he was charged with its theft. The charges read that the equipment was worth some twenty-six thousand pounds. My evidence to the court, which was accepted, was that the equipment was nearly worthless (the rusty motherboards, for example, were brought into court), although I did put a nominal value of one thousand pounds on it in case one or two of the working items could be used as spares.

This case also had an interesting drama on the side. It was about to start when it was discovered the judge, who was a recorder, had been acting in the same court in Carlisle as a counsel on a case during the previous week, and the jury was the same. This caused the case to be postponed at the eleventh hour.

I only got to know after arriving home from London, having interrupted an assignment there. Furthermore, on arriving at Manchester, I had booked my rail tickets to Carlisle for the next morning. I was therefore faced, through no fault of my own, with the cost of my abortive return journey from London to Manchester and the Carlisle tickets plus the blanking out of what could have been a fee-earning day.

Although instructing solicitors normally paid one's fees and expenses, those for actually giving evidence in court were paid by the court itself. Initially, Carlisle Crown Court refused to pay for the losses I had incurred, and I had ironically practically to go to court to get them to pay up.

A second case I was involved in, where the Prosecution exaggerated the evidence concerned a Defendant who was charged with possessing indecent images of children on his computer and a CD. My forensic examination showed that these figures were only reached if duplicate copies of a particular still or video image were included, and most, if not all, this duplication was caused by the computer itself making back-up copies.

My evidence, which was accepted by the Court, reduced the numbers in the charges by at least a factor of four. The duplication was indisputable because identical files have the same hash number. A hash number is a figure created by an algorithm using the contents of the file as its input, and the FTK software calculated the hash number.

That the Prosecution did not take account of this was surprising because their numbers were supplied by an IT company, which offered forensic services. Even more surprising was this IT company presumed to calibrate the degree of paedophilia depicted in each image.

Although Rosemary did not see the images, she did see the file names as she typed my report. She found even these revolting as I also did.

As well as exaggerations of evidence, the police also, on one occasion, blatantly disregarded the requirements of PACE. PACE requires that a mirror image be taken of any computer media, particularly a hard drive. Any forensic investigation is then conducted on copies of this mirror image so that the original is not corrupted in any way. This effectively precludes the original computer from being used.

This was the case concerning a defendant who was charged with benefit fraud. During the trial, the original computer was held as evidence in a room adjacent to the courtroom. During the recess, in contravention of the PACE rules, the police witnesses attending the court switched the computer on and opened a folder named "secret", which, as it happened, contained copies of the forged identification documents, which had been used in the fraud. Not only was this contrary to PACE rules, it occurred when I was attending the court, yet the prosecution did not inform me until after the event. Surprisingly, the judge allowed the trial to proceed despite the defence counsel's protests. I would have expected the case to go to appeal, but I heard nothing further.

I was also an expert witness in a further case of apparent police malpractice. A defendant for whom I acted in a previous case asked for me again. The previous case in West Yorkshire involved his being charged with having indecent images on his computer of underage children. When the so-called indecent images were examined, it turned out the only one that could be so construed was of a fifteen-year-old girl showing one nipple.

The new case was somewhat puzzling. He claimed the two cases were part of a pattern of police harassment because he was writing a book to expose an illegal covert British Army operation in Africa. Whether this was true or whether he was a fantasist, I was never able to determine, but he was a paraplegic in a wheelchair as a result of injuries suffered, he said, during military service.

As part of their investigations into the second case, the police, in this case, Devon and Cornwall Constabulary, had seized his laptop, which he claimed contained the draft of the book. The police claimed they had only switched the computer on for only two or three minutes. However, the CMOS battery on the laptop was dead.

The CMOS battery is not the main battery on a personal or laptop computer but the one that should operate continuously so that the computer retains, amongst other things, the date and time. If it goes dead, the date and time revert to midnight at the start of the first of January 1984.

However, on examining the laptop, I discovered a number of files with dates and times of up to ninety minutes after midnight on the first of January 1984. This, in my opinion, indicated that the computer had been switched on for considerably longer than the two or three minutes claimed by the police whilst it was in their custody, there being evidence that the CMOS battery was not dead when they seized the laptop. How this influenced the court proceedings I did not find out, nor what the case was really about, nor the outcome as I was only paid to attend the court, which was in Plymouth for one day. This lack of feedback was typical of the behaviour of many instructing solicitors.

As I approached sixty-five and was contemplating my retirement, I needed to take a decision on my idea whether to turn Price Project Services as a computer forensic services provider but with others taking an increasing role. As mentioned above, there were, however, significant drawbacks. Also, there was a move for expert witnesses generally to be accredited with all the hassle that would involve.

What finally decided against me pursuing the idea was my final case. A Manchester-based solicitor for whom I had previously worked on a couple of cases, although it was based in Kent, brought this to me.

The defendant was charged with strangling his estranged partner. The computer element was that the prosecution was alleging that it was premeditated on the basis that the defendant's computer showed he had googled on it "how to murder your partner", "strangulation", and other seemingly relevant terms.

As usual, the prosecution only released the mirror image of the relevant hard drive and other media close to the date of the trial and then in dribs and drabs. A further complication was that Kent Constabulary had significant computer expertise. Indeed, they had produced a forensic tool, which they marketed, that listed all the internet searches on a device even if they had been deleted, and I had to purchase that tool and familiarise myself with it.

The report I produced explained these difficulties, including the lateness of the hour I had been supplied with the evidence. Unfortunately, putting this in my expert report did not endear me to my instructing solicitor. What I concluded was that in the two years life of the hard drive, something of the order of a quarter of a million Google searches had been undertaken across a variety of topics, and this put into context the twelve or so the prosecution had selectively produced in evidence.

Even some of these could not necessarily be relevant to the alleged crime; for example, searches for "strangler" led to the website of an acid rock band of that name.

I was asked to attend the trial on a particular day when the computer aspects of the case were to be dealt with. I travelled from Manchester to Maidstone the day before and stayed overnight. The prosecution police computer expert gave evidence, and in response to my point about the number of Google searches compared to those that were relevant, introduced for the first time the possibility that the defendant could have deleted some relevant ones in a way that the Kent Constabulary forensic software could not detect. He did not, however, provide any evidence that this had been done.

There was indeed some general-purpose software on the hard drive, which could have done this, but this was the first time such a possibility had been introduced. I pointed this out when I was asked to comment and added that I could not give chapter and verse on whether it had been done or not without further forensic investigation.

There was neither the time nor the facilities on the day I was allocated to attend the trial, and my offer to do so as soon as possible was ignored, and I was dismissed. Nevertheless, this new possibility had been put before the jury without warning and without adequate analysis, and I was surprised the judge allowed it to be admitted.

Overall, this and the stress the day induced in me decided me against any further expert witness work despite the remuneration. Another lesser factor was the setting up of a quango to regulate expert witnesses, and I was reluctant to effectively have to re-qualify as well as having to pay a substantial fee.

CHAPTER 23

INTO EUROPE

Early in the 1990s, the UK government decided that rather than funding UK research themselves, it made sense to encourage those UK organisations wanting public sector financial support to seek it from the various European Commission Schemes. They saw this as a mechanism for getting back from Brussels some of the UK contribution to the European Union Budget.

The European Commission Schemes generally followed the UK collaborative research model of programmes on specific themes. This was not surprising because many of the Commission staff working in the area were ex UK civil servants and academics that had been involved in the UK system. The European schemes were batched into "Frameworks", which were announced and launched every few years.

The fourth of these "Frameworks", which had a budget of 1.9 billion euros, was concerned with research into Systems Engineering. To assist its formulation, a working group of industrialists was set up, and I was asked to be its rapporteur.

The working group met on several occasions in 1994, and I duly produced a report detailing its conclusions. I was therefore somewhat frustrated when, although there had been no criticism of my work, a final version was produced by the Commission's officials, which bore little resemblance to what I had written and what the working group had discussed and decided.

This led me to the decision that although working for the Commission added to my curriculum vitae, I would not undertake any more work for them whilst more rewarding opportunities were available. Although the absence of feeling that one was doing anything useful was paramount, the poor fee levels and inadequate expenses for overnight stays in Brussels did not enamour me to Commission assignments. Particularly I recall having to stay in a very low-grade hotel characterised by peeling wallpaper, etc.

Another factor was the contradictory approach of the Commission to value for money. They insisted that one took the cheapest flights, which meant, of course, that they could not be open tickets. However, when one pointed out that it was necessary to leave to catch one's designated flight back to the UK, they would inevitably ask that one stay on, which meant, of course, re-booking a full fair ticket. To add insult to injury, the expenses department quibbled about paying for tickets for both the cancelled and the actual flights. Apparently, this was the experience of many working on assignments for the Commission.

My assignment for the Commission also had an interesting aftermath. My invoice naturally had Value Added Tax (VAT) included, which the Commission refused to pay. However, the local UK VAT office insisted that I had to charge it, pointing out a clause in their rules which said that VAT was chargeable on work done for an overseas national government or local authority body. However, I pointed out that the Commission was a supranational body, and therefore the clause did not apply. Fortunately, my interpretation proved to be right, and PPSL avoided charging VAT.

Following this assignment with the European Commission, I was not short of more rewarding opportunities; therefore, despite being asked, I did not undertake any further assignments directly with them. However, there were two further occasions when I was involved with the European Commission, albeit indirectly.

The first of these was when one of the companies involved in the Management of Information programme asked me to chair a workshop they were conducting for the Commission in Brussels. This I agreed to do but made the mistake of scheduling it on my way back from one of my regular Greek Island holidays. What I did not think through was the shock to my system of going from lotus-eating on a remote Greek Island to chairing a workshop with delegates from over 20 countries with simultaneous translation in the space of three days. However, I managed to avoid any faux pas such as cracking xenophobic jokes and generally, I performed the task to the satisfaction of those attending.

The assignment, however, increased my cynicism of the European Commission and its officials. Rosemary was accompanying me, and we were to take the Eurostar back to London early on the Friday evening. Unfortunately, a number of taxi companies and taxis we hailed refused to take us the short trip to Brussels Midi Station. They were all only interested in more lucrative fares taking Commission officials to the airport for flights to their home countries. Eventually, we just entered a taxi before the driver asked us for a destination and simply refused to budge until he took us. Fortunately, we made the last Eurostar, which connected with the last train we could catch from London to Manchester that evening.

Ever since our first meeting at Salford University, the pro vice-chancellor for research, Professor Peter Brandon, had wanted me to get involved with Salford, and the opportunity arose in 2006. It consisted of a part-time senior research fellow position with part-time meaning one day a week for some two years. The post was in the School of the Built Environment and specifically in the Think Laboratory, a discussion/educational facility utilising the very latest technology and specifically virtual reality. I reported to Professor Terence Fernando, a world-renowned expert on virtual reality.

Amongst his many research projects and grants was a "network of excellence" on virtual reality called INTUITION funded by the European Commission.

INTUITION had around sixty participating organisations, industrial and academic, spread over nearly all the member nations of the European Union, and it was coordinated by the Institute of Communications and Computer Systems of the National Technical University of Athens.

Liaising with so many participants and meeting the reporting requirements, particularly financial, of the European Commission as interpreted by the coordinators was mind-blowingly complex beyond the available resources of the University, so most of my time at Salford was not spent doing research but instead addressing these administrative issues.

However, there was one area where I contributed away from the administrative bureaucracy - Salford were charged with defining and possibly producing a common virtual reality infrastructure platform for the Network. Time meant I could only address the definition aspects, and as it was not clear that I was actually supposed to be producing an infrastructure platform, this seemed to satisfy them.

It was interesting that as well as the ambiguity as to whether a definition or an actual product was required, generally, the definition of what was required was largely gobbledygook, more so than could be explained by the language differences of the authors.

Inevitably, the geographic spread of the participants in INTUITION required me to indulge in some foreign travel, and thus I visited Rome, Berne and Athens in the course of my participation. The last enabled me to visit Kalymnos after a week's work in Athens. Naturally, this was at my own expense, although this was not significant because my Greek friends were so pleased to see me that I was not charged for accommodation or meals.

CHAPTER 24

THINKING, WRITING AND SPEAKING

My book on managing computer projects, which I referred to in a previous chapter, encapsulated my thinking in 1984, the year it was written, on how computer projects should be conducted. This was based on the waterfall model of software development, where the feasibility study is completed before the requirements are designed, the requirements are completed before the programming commences, and so on.

However, I had begun to realise that in many cases, despite the waterfall model being at the heart of many standards, contracts, etc, it was not very realistic. Therefore I attempted to promote, both in writing and speaking, more realistic models of system and particularly software development.

The most significant attempt was in the form of a second book which I wrote around 2003 called *"Unreal IT Why?"* viz *"Unreality"*, which recommended a much more pragmatic approach to the topic. It was a combination of my own experience and good academic research. However, the publishers I approached failed to appreciate this and were only interested in it if it were an academic textbook or a practical book, and so I failed to get it published.

A major motivation for the writing of both books and much of my parallel writing and speaking was to address the very high failure rate of IT projects. I used extensively the worldwide headlines (See Appendix II) about IT disaster projects to publicise my efforts. Notwithstanding my efforts and several others internationally, the high failure rate of IT projects continued unabated, and my attention switched to why society continued to make the same mistakes. My conclusions were twofold:

- The originators of such projects are either too arrogant to learn from the experience of others or, in some cases, even their own.
- There is something "weird" about IT and particularly software projects.

The situation was not helped by many observers drawing attention to the first cause and then, in some cases promoting their own ideas, worthy as some of these are, and not being aware of the second issue.

Another of my attempts to address the problem of the high failure rates of IT projects was a seminar, "*Dependability: For the People, By the People*", organised under the auspices of The Software Reliability and Metrics Club.

This was a one-day event in Central London and, in spite of a list of speakers that included such luminaries as my expert witness colleague, Professor John Buxton, and Professor Ian Somerville, author of the best-selling book "*Software Engineering*", it was extremely poorly attended. Fortunately, Professor Tom Anderson, the chairman of the club, was quite forgiving.

Tom was not always so forgiving. I had been invited to be the after-dinner speaker at the club's annual conference banquet, and rather than keeping the style of speaking light, as required of after-dinner speaking, I used it as a rant against the then in-trouble new

London Air Traffic Control Centre Project which, given my previous background, meant I was particularly critical.

This criticism I also put in an article which the Guild of Air Traffic Control Officers solicited for their journal "*Transmit*". Here I predicted the new centre would never work; therefore, I should have egg on my face when it eventually apparently did. However, in my defence, the project overran its budget by 100% and was five years late. It also failed to provide a 60% increase in maximum air traffic throughput, which was the intended target.

The target itself was, in fact, rather dubious, having been picked from the air after a boozy lunch by an MIT research (Mitre) consultant advising the UK National Air Traffic Services. In fact, his prediction was heavily caveated, but this was ignored when the project was initially justified.

There were lighter moments involving speaking at club events. On one occasion, I introduced a talk by justifying myself as being an expert on safety by the number of disasters I had been adjacent to at the time. As I went through the list commencing with the Three Mile Island Disaster (see Chapter 14), I became aware of the audience starting to snigger.

As I was not intending to be funny, I was somewhat bemused, but all was soon explained. Tom Anderson, who was chairing the session, had crawled off the stage, sensing I might cause a disaster there and then.

Nevertheless, Tom was percipient because sometime later, he was my guest at a Lake District weekend meeting of the Manchester Pedestrians walking club. A group of us had climbed Haystacks, and Tom had given me a lift. Because of my girth and hence slowness, we were the last twosome to leave the car park at Buttermere to return to the hotel north of Keswick. We had, in fact, not reached the exit to the car park when a troublesome sound came from underneath the bonnet and Tom's car juddered to a halt. The timing chain had gone, and the car was immobile. It being late on Saturday and the rest of the party well on their way back to the hotel, we appeared stranded; however, miraculously, a local farmer's wife managed to squash my girth into a Riley Elf (an upmarket mini) and gave us a lift back to the hotel where we just made dinner on time.

My speaking engagements on safety were not just confined to the UK. I was invited to speak at a European Safety Critical event in Paris which gave me the opportunity of taking my mother. She was then in her mid-eighties and had always yearned to visit Paris, but until then had not done so.

Rosemary accompanied us, kindly looking after Mum whilst I was engaged at the event. She really enjoyed her trip, with one exception. We travelled by Eurostar and whilst transiting the Channel Tunnel she went to the toilet. Unfortunately, rather than pressing the flush lever, she pressed the emergency one. Fortunately, she regained her place in the carriage before two train attendants arrived, summoned by the loud klaxon, and no further damage was done.

Another vehicle for my views on systems and software development was my ad hoc or regular lectures at various universities. The most cogent of these was at Lancaster University in 2004/5 under the heading "*The Forty Years War – Stan Price v IT*".

This chronicled my controversial thought processes over my career to date and how they had transitioned from the formal waterfall model to the people-centric approach, which I then and now advocate. A subplot was swipes in the form of several cartoons (See Appendix II) at those who advocated silver bullet solutions to the systems development problem.

My pontificating on the failure of IT projects even led to an appearance on BBC Breakfast Television commenting on yet another large UK public sector IT project failure.

To be fair, it was not just in the UK that these appeared but was and is, of course, an international phenomenon. Furthermore, it is probable the private sector has an equal number of such failures, the only difference being those in the private sector are less publicised. The television interview was interesting in that the BBC insisted it was conducted with a desktop computer staged besides me.

Safety and the systems development process were not the only topics of my public speaking. I gave a talk at the annual software testing conference organised by the British Computer Society, which I was asked to repeat at an international software testing conference in Washington, DC.

This I jazzed up a little, including a throwaway line that Americans were not necessarily comfortable with technology. I cited the Boston Tea Party and the foolhardiness of putting tea in cold water. It is to the credit of the American audience that they found my remarks humorous as they were indeed intended.

Humour played a part in much of my public speaking. In this, I was fortunate that I remembered a significant repertoire of jokes and humorous anecdotes and had even invented some. Many of these exceeded the ever-increasing boundary of political correctness, but in the main, rarely did my audiences raise objections.

Speaking assignments occasionally threw up surprises. Once, at a security conference whilst talking about passwords, I pontificated that they should have some meaning to their owner whilst being otherwise extremely obscure. As an example, I mentioned a friend who used a password composed of the initials of the West Bromwich Albion Football Club forwards in 1927. To my surprise, one of my audience shouted out the five names.

In parallel with my speaking, I also had a number of articles published in various journals. Additionally, I contributed several regular articles to a computer newsletter called Datalink, but here the topics were largely chosen for me. What was interesting about this was that I was paid ten pence per word, which resulted in a rather verbose style of writing. This contrasted with my writing in the other domains in which I worked, covering expert witness statements; technical reports; the odd academic paper, as well as these journalistic efforts where a quote was de rigueur.

Indeed, the different styles required I found quite fascinating and whatever the format as well as the prime purpose of writing, they were also useful in helping me sort out my thinking. Also, I found sorting out my ideas and getting them down on paper was therapeutic.

Some of my thinking and writing lead me to investigate a number of business ideas. For one assignment for Salford University, I invented a series of cartoon characters parodying various disciplines within the IT industry – e.g. the introverted programmer who codes all day and hacks all night.

It occurred to me that if puppets representing these characters could be produced, one might make educational videos using them. I got as far as talking to a puppet manufacturer who shared the same building, but that was as far as it got.

Another idea was to set up an online database of advice on topics connected to the IT development process, which could be accessed for a charge by those needing guidance. This got as far as a prototype produced by one of my Sheffield students on secondment to PPSL, but eventually, I took the project no further.

As I neared retirement, I started a variant on my speaking events. I began giving talks to Rotary and Probus events with basically two standard offerings. One was an extension of my IT talks, but in a more humorous vein called "*Great Computer Cock Ups*". This included anecdotes such as the computerised toilets on Pedolino trains, which locked the doors when the retention tanks were full, irrespective of whether there was someone in the toilet or not.

The other offering was on the Kennedy Space Flight Centre, with which I was familiar from my time in the USA.

Stan Price

CHAPTER 25

PLANES, BOATS, TRAINS AND CARS

Inevitably, my career has involved much more travelling than if I'd had conventional nine to five occupations. Apart from the advantage of visiting exciting and attractive locations in the UK and worldwide, generally it assisted my interest in some modes of travel. I was, of course, always interested in trains since childhood, but my employment with Hawker Siddeley and subsequently the Civil Aviation Authority generated an interest in aviation.

Perhaps I became too interested as I was often castigated for being a bore by, for instance, drinking companions on the Thames Chiswick towpath as I commentated on the continuous flow of airliners approaching Heathrow.

The interest extended to me starting to learn to fly. This was mainly whilst I was in the USA, where it was considerably cheaper. Unfortunately, I did not pursue it to the extent of obtaining my pilot's licence or even going solo, but I did clock up several hours on single-engined light aircraft.

My first ever flight as a passenger was a business trip from Manchester to Heathrow while I was with Hawker Siddeley. The aircraft was a four turboprop Vickers Vanguard. As described in Chapter 9, this was followed by several trips in the company's aircraft.

Also, when visiting Hawker Siddeley's Kingston plant, I would finish by having drinks with old college friends in Shepperton. I would then take a taxi to Heathrow and board the last flight of the day to Manchester. This was invariably a British Airways three-engined Trident, which stopped overnight in Manchester before being scheduled on the early morning Paris departure.

Otherwise, the majority of UK internal travel, apart from business trips to Northern Ireland and sometimes Scotland, was by rail; however, one notable exception was when I managed to finish a meeting in Plymouth at 2 pm and then make a 7 pm speaking engagement in Oldham. This involved flying from Plymouth to Heathrow with a short stopover at Newquay and then taking the Shuttle to Manchester.

My trips to the USA whilst employed by the CAA and the police, of course, involved transatlantic flights. Initially, the aircraft involved were VC10s, but later they were all Boeings.

Being employed by the CAA meant, until security was beefed up after the increase in terrorist attacks, I could often ride in the cockpit. The most notable of these was the last commercial flight of a BOAC Rolls-Royce engined Boeing 707 (707-436).

I also flew in the cockpit from Athens to Gatwick on the last commercial flight of a Comet. This was operated by the long-defunct Dan-Air, but it was not on this occasion a business trip.

Flying on business on two occasions got me in trouble with my employers. Once was the helicopter trip over Manhattan described in Chapter 12. And more serious was the one concerning my trip to the USA on behalf of the Metropolitan Police when I was accused of living it up on the taxpayer, as described in Chapter 14.

Long-distance journeys around the USA were almost inevitably by air, the only exception being by train on Amtrak between Newark and Philadelphia.

Several of my business trips involved a combination of air and rail, most notably when I was asked to speak at Univac's European Management Centre in the picturesque Saint-Paul-de-Vence in southern France. Other commitments meant I had to fly back from Nice to Manchester, changing flights in Zurich, but the outward journey was by the more leisurely night sleeper from Calais to Nice. The highlight of this was the view of the floodlit Sacré Coeur in Paris as the train reversed at the Gare du Nord.

The use of night sleeper trains generally featured a lot in early business travelling. Including whilst working at Woodford, my return journeys from evenings socialising in Central London, as described in Chapter 7.

Not all such journeys were pleasant. Once, after a monitoring meeting in Plymouth, I travelled up to London on the sleeper for an early morning meeting the next day. I was suffering from flu, and in the loneliness of my compartment, I seemed to get worse, so much so I nearly decamped and got medical assistance at Bristol. In the event, I soldiered on, and I believe I performed reasonably the next day.

My most common train journey by far and mainly on business was between Manchester and London, and I estimate the number of times I have made the journey runs well into the four figures. Inevitably, I got to know many of the regular rail staff and particularly those in the dining car. On one memorable occasion, I was sat opposite the then Labour cabinet minister and Member of Parliament for a Manchester Constituency, Gerald Kaufmann. To my delight, the staff ignored him and, focussing on me, asked, "Your usual bottle of Chardonnay, Mr Price?" Quite a contrast from my days as a tea boy.

On another occasion, I was seated opposite the then Chief Constable of Greater Manchester Police, Sir James Anderton. At the time, he was highly controversial for, amongst other things, claiming he talked to God. So him talking to me was rather exalting.

My interest in, and knowledge of railways helped in the planning of my business trips. One example was getting from Manchester to Melton Mowbray. I knew one early Manchester to London train stopped at Nuneaton, where I could connect with a cross-country train from Birmingham to Cambridge, which stopped at Melton Mowbray. As well as making for a fast journey, it enabled me to have a proper breakfast on the London train, which I could not have done by a more conventional route.

Apart from train travel fitting in with my interest in railways, the ability to work on the move that train travel facilitated was of considerable benefit in maximising what Price Project Services offered its clients both in terms of cost as well as quality.

Even when I had the use of a laptop, working on the train required a significant amount of space, which outstripped what was normally available in Standard Class. Therefore on long journeys, I inevitably travelled first class. Travelling in standard class reduced my ability to work on the train and contributed to a longer working day. As I charged my clients for my time, my travelling Standard would often mean an increased charge to them that was much more than paying the First Class increment.

This caused a hiatus on the occasion of an early tax inspection of PPSL. The inspector concerned had the temerity to query why I cited breakfast on the train as a working expense and suggested I took sandwiches. I pointed out that I was not prepared to extend an excessively long working day by spending time preparing sandwiches. Furthermore, I demanded to see what the Inland Revenue staff regulations had to say about allowable expenses for someone of my grade. At this, he backed down.

Later, there were more and more attempts to restrict first-class train travel, particularly by the TSB, and I countered by pointing out that making me travel second-class would actually cost them more.

I also pointed out that I used and claimed for the cheapest tickets by booking in advance, and in my final years, my senior railcard came into play.

The proximity of my home to Central Manchester greatly facilitated the use of trains for business travel on behalf of PPSL, so much so that I rarely used road transport apart from taxis from home to Piccadilly or Victoria Rail Stations or to the airport.

The number of such journeys was so frequent that the black cab drivers who took me home from the rank at Piccadilly Station got to know me, and before I could give my destination, they would say "the big tree on Hazelbottom Rd".

My travelling was so extensive that I believe I could not have undertaken all I did if I had used cars, not to mention the impact on my health.

Prior to PPSL, I used my own cars extensively on Hawker Siddeley business, while the Metropolitan Police provided a car and driver. Software Sciences insisted I use my company car even when public transport was much more sensible. The most exotic vehicle I used was the hired Oldsmobile Cutlass Supreme, which the CAA provided me with in the States.

Travel over water was even less frequent and was confined to the Channel Crossing for the Saint-Paul-de-Vance assignment referred to above and the Lake Windermere crossing described in Chapter 13.

Stan Price

CHAPTER 26

GOD AND/OR THE CHURCH

As described in previous chapters, I was brought up in the Church of England and was a regular churchgoer at the local St Thomas's. I was also involved in regular church-related activities such as participating in the Whit Monday walks of witness, both around the parish and also in the main multi-church walk in central Manchester.

In later years this took the form of playing a side drum. However, this involvement in the Church was in the way of a habit rather than any deep belief, although I never challenged this part of my upbringing. Hence, when I went up to University, I never bothered with a church in London. Incidentally, being a student at Kings London with its religious foundations, I had the opportunity of undertaking a course, which along with a degree, would qualify me for Associateship of Kings College (AKC). However, this would have meant my having to attend lectures at 9 am on Mondays, a not very appealing prospect, from which I refrained.

What I did do was say my prayers almost every night. These generally consisted of asking God for the well-being of my parents, brother and whoever the current girlfriend was. There were also other specific requests, but I never asked for anything trivial such as a Manchester City victory.

I had, however, thought out a personal morality. One part of this was based on my father's dictum of always telling the truth. Another part was doing and saying what I believed to be true, irrespective of how this impacted my personal advancement and career. Although I first thought this through and started attempting to adhere to it whilst working for the Civil Aviation Authority, it was really tested in my Sales and Marketing role at Software Sciences. Here, the tweaking, without lying, of curriculum vitae to emphasise a certain consultant's suitability for a particular assignment was a regular occurrence.

A third part of my creed involved God in the sense that one was born with a set of abilities, and it was incumbent on one to maximise them to the full. This included making decisions between good and evil.

My first serious brush with religion came with my "breakdown" at the time of my father's death and my return to Manchester. The prospect of there being a God was, as mentioned previously, a very therapeutic concept and helped in no small way to assist my recovery. This was particularly so of the idea of there being a superior being on whom one could share one's problems via prayer.

I returned to discover St Thomas's itself had gone through a difficult time. An arson attack had severely damaged the church and made it unusable. Services were therefore being held in my old primary school, which was adjacent. Although the church was under-insured, key members of the congregation had organised its rebuilding using labour from a community youth training scheme. While this rebuilding was taking place, I was asked if I would be one of the two churchwardens, and I accepted.

Initially, as a churchwarden, I was primarily concerned with the rebuilding of the church. This was an uplifting task for, with some notable exceptions, it brought the whole Church and neighbouring community together towards a common purpose. This was so striking that I could almost advocate that every church should have a fire, say every twenty-five years.

The exceptions to this was a very small clique, who took a reactionary attitude to every suggested change that took advantage of the situation to improve, particularly the fabric of the church. The most notable of these was the replacement of old uncomfortable fixed pews with modern upholstered seats. Fortunately, a new clergyman with the title of rector, who had been inducted after the fire, brushed aside these objections.

It was not only the reactionary posture that was a problem. One of the clique wanted to be involved in everything but had neither the time nor the skills in many areas to meet the commitments involved, so in order that she did not become a bottleneck, one had to curb their aspirations.

The other significant problem was the necessary but unprofessional role of the officers of the diocese of Manchester. One specific major difficulty centred around the new heating system. The architect employed by the church was an advocate of overhead gas-fired radiation heating. He convinced me that this was a good idea on the basis of simple physics.

St Thomas's Church, like so many Victorian churches, was a barn-like building that cost significant funds to heat, despite only being used two or three times a week. The high cost was caused significantly by the conventional convection heating having to heat the vast volume of air within the church. Radiation heating, however, would not heat this body of air but only the people and artefacts on which it radiated, and therefore was a much more economical proposition.

The relevant diocesan official was, however, quite opposed to this break with conventional church heating, and his opposition was significantly delaying the completion of the rebuilding. Our disagreement culminated in a telephone call between us. I was feeding a coin box in a telephone booth on Great Malvern Station - I had business at the Royal Radar and Signals Research Establishment, and he was in his Manchester Office.

Despite his knowing where I was and the constraints on the conversation, he kept on raising spurious objections, so much so that I said we would go ahead with the radiation heating anyway. His riposte was that he washed his hands of the matter, and if there were any problems, it was down to the parish.

The church rebuilding thus proceeded with our choice of heating. To my view, the overall outcome was both aesthetically and practically more than satisfactory. Visually the old-style white roof and brown beams contrasted most effectively with the red upholstered chairs and the red carpets at floor level with the light sanded pulpit.

Once the church was re-dedicated and in use normally, my role as churchwarden should have reverted to routine leadership and administration. However, it was not to be. The new rector had, perhaps understandably, put tremendous effort into the rebuilding. This included manual labour, sandpapering furniture and the like.

However, once the church was re-opened, his supposedly primary spiritual and pastoral work came under scrutiny. Unfortunately, his acerbic domineering style alienated many of the congregation. This came to a head when for one service, I was the only member of the congregation. Clearly, something had to be done, and it was the duty of the churchwardens to take the initiative.

However, before taking action, I consulted another clergyman who had been on the same induction course as the rector. He informed me that the rector's personality problems had manifested themselves even then, and it appeared remarkable that he had, in fact, been ordained.

After unsuccessfully attempting to discuss the problems with the rector and although sympathetic to him at a personal level, for the general sake of the church, he had to go. My fellow churchwarden and I therefore approached the Area Dean. A major part of the rector's problem was drink.

We were amazed to discover that the Area Dean and the church hierarchy were aware of the situation, and for reasons best known to themselves, had done nothing about it. We then made our concerns official, and as a result, they eventually took action, and the rector left the Parish. Sadly, some months later, he passed away.

Although not my problems as a warden, there was an issue with the wider local church that resulted in a very jaundiced view of the Church of England generally.

The local area had a number of Church of England Parishes. One nearby parish normally had very low attendance figures, yet the church building was approaching cathedral proportions and was in an extremely poor state of repair. Understandably, the loyal regular churchgoers wanted it to stay open, although its upkeep was irreconcilable with its income.

The diocese decided that it would be kept open with a grant from the Heritage Fund subject to its becoming, in addition to a church, a local music centre. Many felt this was an extremely dubious proposition and was simply postponing the closure, yet the diocese persisted, and it remained open, and the music centre idea was pursued.

My efforts involved in the church rebuilding and the strain of the rector issue coupled with my jaundiced view of the church generally after some six or seven years led me to the conclusion that it was time for me to relinquish the churchwarden role. So I resigned without any animosity insofar as I know, from any members of the parish.

Thereafter, initially, I confined my relationship with the Church to attending high and feast day services and financial support. After some years, the then-current rector (the second after the tragic one) instituted a Wednesday lunchtime communion service followed by a simple lunch. This was weekly during Lent and monthly throughout the rest of the year. By then, I had started to work from home, and it was therefore convenient for me to attend, so I did.

The year 2010 saw me totally reducing my work commitments, and it coincided with the rector who had initiated the Wednesday lunch services moving on. Because of the lack of sufficient members of the congregation willing and able to perform roles within the parish, he had been partly performing the work of treasurer, and as I had time on my hands, I offered to help by taking on the post fully after he left. The Parochial Church Council, in the main, were more than pleased to accept my offer.

Immediately, it became apparent that there were anomalies in the way the financial affairs of the parish had been conducted. One of these was that there were inaccuracies between the records of monies collected during services and what was banked. Until I put in place a proper system, I had to spend an inordinate amount of time performing forensic accounting in order to see there was a proper audit trail.

Another, perhaps more serious problem was that for three years, the parish had collected monies to be dispensed to charities, but these had not been passed on. If this had been reported to the tax and the charities authorities, the parish could have faced severe penalties, so I immediately ensured the charities were paid what they were owed.

My task in addressing these and other problem was not helped by sheer obstructionism on the part of one of the churchwardens. She was one of those who had exhibited the same negative characteristics at the time of the church rebuilding after the fire. One example of her obstructionism was her refusal to hand over the cheque book for the parish accounts until ordered to do so by the Area Dean.

Even though I was treasurer, because of my previous experiences, I tried to keep myself at arm's length from the parish, but inevitably,

I got more and more sucked in. For example, when the opportunity arose to fill the vacant organist position but the parish could not reasonably afford it, I offered anonymously to pay half his fees.

For the first couple of years, the parish was without a rector, and I was appalled to learn how the diocese planned to fill the position. Their idea was that as well as there being a joint rector of St Thomas's and Trinity Church on Cheetham Hill, there was to be the added responsibility of the church referred to earlier.

This was the one which had been to turn it into a music centre. Predictably, this venture had failed after the wasted expenditure of hundreds of thousands of pounds. Any new incumbent was therefore faced with the difficulties of coping with the closure of this church and parish and the unusual and difficult situation at Trinity. This was because Trinity was an uneasy collaboration between the Church of England and the United Reform Church with their different types of churchmanship and administrative arrangements.

A third difficulty was the reactionary clique at St Thomas's with its uncooperative attitude and stifling control of all things non-financial. It may well have been that those in the diocese taking these decisions were unaware of the difficulties, particularly in the latter case, but anyone who was aware would have realised that the job was mission impossible for whoever took it on. I, however, perhaps unwisely, decided to help whoever took the post.

However impossible the mission was, the lady who took the post made an excellent attempt at it, despite being involved in a serious car accident early in her incumbency. The unviable church was closed, and its parish was merged with the parish of St Luke's, which was the Church of England element of Trinity. Additionally, the problems of Trinity initially seemed relatively under control.

Meanwhile, at St Thomas's, under her leadership, the backlog of infrastructure and administrative issues that had resulted from the unnecessary bottleneck of the controlling church clique wanting to have a say in everything whilst being incapable of carrying many of them out were progressively addressed. The overgrown grounds were tidied up, the church redecorated (it had not been done since the fire), and the accumulated detritus that had accumulated inside the church was sorted out. The last was so bad it was found that one storage cupboard was maggot-infested.

For my part, as well as my treasurer duties, I got myself elected to the Parochial Church Council (PCC), so I could expedite repairs to the roof, which had been leaking for some years. As well as my desire to help, I did this to overcome my frustration about the procrastinating of those who should have been handling the matter.

Part of the process in getting things moving was the appointment of a new churchwarden for the post who was not part of the reactionary clique. The PCC, therefore, passed a resolution that the parish would fall in line with the general Church of England rule that churchwarden's terms of office should last no longer than six years - the incumbent churchwarden had served much longer than that.

Unfortunately, she obtained a statement from the assistant diocesan solicitor that the six years started from the date of the resolution, and she was therefore entitled to stay in post until then. She kept this to herself for several months before announcing it just prior to the Annual Parish Meeting when elections took place, and it was unlikely that anyone else would put themselves forward for the post.

I therefore obtained a copy of the church rulings on the matter and felt they indicated that this interpretation of the rules was incorrect, and accordingly, I sought the advice of the diocesan solicitor herself. She confirmed that her assistant's ruling was incorrect, and the churchwarden could not stand again.

The individual took exception to the change. This was not conducive to the well-being of the Rector after the efforts she had put in rejuvenating the Parish.

Her situation was soon made even more difficult when stonework fell from the tower of the Trinity church. This was a symptom of much more serious structural problems about which discussions had dragged on for a number of years. Not only was this a problem in itself, a figure of half a million pounds being bandied around as the cost of rectification, but also the issue caused the differences between the Church of England and URC elements at Trinity to widen. Understandably, this new stress and the historic ones tolled on the rector who, after a period of sick leave, took early retirement.

Incredibly, a significant number of the members of the parish appeared to accept what had happened to their rector with few or no recriminations against the clique who had partly caused it. This was so repugnant to me that despite my own and my family's near century-long association with the parish, I severed all connections with it. This included removing from my will a significant bequest to the parish. As chance would have it, a close friend, albeit a lay reader, acted as incumbent at my father's old parish in Salford, and it seemed sensible to go there for my infrequent church attendances.

Despite my negative experiences of the parish and the Church generally, I was determined that they should not influence my personal deliberations on the existence of God. To assist these, apart from the many marvellous things she had done for the church, the rector was personally helpful to me in qualifying my agnosticism.

Although still an agnostic, I believe it irrefutable that Jesus Christ existed and what he taught is largely consistent with my own sense of morality. This is, I believe, a reasoned view not just brought about by my childhood and later environment. I therefore can subscribe to one-third of the Christian Trinity. The other two thirds I still have difficulty accepting, although generally, I sense there is a world beyond the merely physical.

Also, given my background as an expert witness, given the number of witnesses to the resurrection, it would probably be accepted as fact in a court of law. Nevertheless, to accept the existence of God fully, I believe I would have to make the leap of faith that many say has to be done or have done. Suffice to say; I am not ready to jump.

Rosemary was very much a practising Christian – she also, at times, was a churchwarden, not the reactionary one, and treasurer and generally helped anyone who needed help. She obviously had a deep faith, and it is to my regret I never significantly discussed it with her.

CHAPTER 27

COMMUNITY ACTIVIST

I not only got involved with causes as part of my professional career but also in a private capacity following my return to Manchester.

The first of these concerned the plan to build houses on the sports ground at the back of my Manchester home. The sports ground was originally for the employees of the Imperial Chemical Industries (ICI) Blackley factory and laboratories. The number of these peaked at approaching ten thousand, but by the end of the twentieth century, this number was much reduced, and the membership of the sports and social club that used the ground largely consisted of local residents.

The sports ground comprised a football and cricket pitch, tennis courts and bowling green and also catered for netball and hockey. It and the hill behind it provided a very pleasant vista from our home, so much so that one could forget one was only two miles from the centre of a major city.

That aside, the sports ground provided happy memories of my childhood, including operating the scoreboard for the almost nightly cricket matches that took place on it during the summer months. The pavilion was also where my parents spent weekend evenings in their latter years and was where I spoke to them on the telephone from the United States, due to their not then having a telephone at home.

The pitches were of a high standard, so much so that the cup semi-finals and finals of nearly all the North Manchester and wider football and cricket competitions were held there. It was also used as the venue for the Manchester Police open day. It was, therefore, a valuable community resource in an area that was starved of them, and it was for this reason, as well as perhaps my own selfish one of preventing the negative impact on my environment, that I got involved in the campaign to save the ground.

At the time, ICI had split into two, and Blackley and hence the ground were owned by the pharmaceuticals half which had been christened Zeneca. Their logic for closing the ground was puzzling. It had a value of in excess of two hundred thousand pounds, but this quadrupled if planning permission for housing on it was obtained. Zeneca had a turnover of billions of pounds, yet according to its management, the whole future of Zeneca was imperilled if the extra monies resulting from the planning permission for housing were not forthcoming.

Manchester City Council supported the housing application, and indeed, some time before, it had designated the land for housing, unbeknown to the local residents. The Council's motivation was to increase the housing stock, and in pursuit of this, they even got Zeneca to increase the housing density in the scheme. Also, Zeneca threatened to re-locate their operations and take away the jobs of the eight hundred who still worked on their Blackley site.

The campaign to save the sports ground thus appeared to be facing an uphill struggle. However, some days before the application was to be heard by the planning committee, a retired ex-ICI senior executive revealed that the Blackley plant processes involved beta-naphthylamine.

This was used as an accelerant in the manufacture of artificial rubber and is a cause of bladder cancer. This was significant because the hill behind the sports ground and our houses was artificial and had been built up from the waste from the ICI Blackley factory.

Occasionally during childhood, against parental instructions, I had ventured onto the hill and recall it consisted of discarded drums, carboys and coke like material with open pools of chemicals In subsequent years the chemical tip, for that was what it was, had not been removed but simply covered over with many layers of earth. Despite this covering the tip, the hill being higher than the sports ground presented a severe risk to the occupants of any housing built on the sports ground, not least by water leaching through in excess of a hundred thousand cubic metres of chemical waste in the tip and onto the site of the sports ground.

Not willing to be reliant on my single source informant, I extensively researched the matter and discovered these health hazards and particularly the risk of bladder cancer, were well known generally in North Manchester.

The existence of the tip was also well known, and the literature for the opening of the Abraham Moss Secondary School, which stands on the hill, acknowledges it is built on a chemical tip.

I also had a personal interest in that a distant American relative had died of cancer having lived on the site of the notorious Love Canal Disaster in Niagara Falls. The disaster involved the construction of a housing estate on the site of a chemical dump and the surfacing of the chemical waste during excessive rainfall leading to the abandonment of the estate and severe health problems for its inhabitants.

Given the health threat posed to any potential residents on the sports ground site, we were confident that the planning application would be rejected and indeed when it came before the Manchester City Council Planning Committee, it was. However, our success was short-lived. At the time of the planning application, the Labour Leader of the City Council and his deputy were away and, for reasons best known to themselves, had the decision reversed on their return, allegedly on the basis of new data. Needless to say, this new data was never revealed.

This reversal did not stop the campaign. By now, we had formed an action group – the Hazelbottom Action Group (HAG) formed of residents and users of the sports ground, particularly the cricket club. We continued to engage with the media, and although we got significant newspaper and radio coverage, strangely enough, the television companies, both BBC and commercial, would not carry the story.

The impact HAG achieved was best indicated by the fact that all prospective parliamentary candidates for the constituency and Zeneca managers attended a public meeting organised by HAG on the eve of the 1997 general election. We also blockaded the site, with, at one point, bulldozers coming within inches of our picket line (which characteristically had Rosemary to the fore). Nevertheless, the use of the land as a sports ground finished, and the clubhouse was destroyed by fire. Zeneca and their contractors blamed this on local vandals, but the timing of the blaze clearly refuted this, as did the attending fire officer.

Eventually, all our efforts proved to be in vain and houses and apartment blocks were built on the site.

All this took place against a backdrop of increasingly more stringent requirements for the investigation of landfill sites, and these required the City Council to investigate the tip. I was promised a copy of the report documenting the result of this investigation, and despite my requesting it for several years, it has never been forthcoming.

Meanwhile, I wait to see in the long term if my concerns for the health of the residents of the houses on the sports ground site were justified. Interestingly, despite Zeneca's use of perpetuating employment as a bargaining chip with the City Council to further their planning applications for both the sports ground and their factory sites, once the planning applications had been approved, they soon totally wound down their north Manchester operations.

The second significant community cause I got involved in was the fight against the closure of our local Metrolink tram stop – Woodlands Road. This was originally a heavy rail station on the third-rail electrified Manchester to Bury line. The Woodlands Road station was six minutes walk from 91 Hazelbottom via an unlit path through some local allotments. Although this reduced its usefulness during the hours of darkness or when the allotment gates were locked - the alternative walk taking double the time, it provided a way of reaching central Manchester by public transport.

There was no bus service in my youth along the valley, including Hazelbottom Road, so the other public transport alternatives were to take a Number 7 bus that crossed the valley to either Rochdale or Cheetham Hill Road, and there change to a second bus, or climb out of the valley on foot to either of the two roads.

Later on, a bus route was introduced along the valley and Hazelbottom Road, but even then, the Woodlands Road stop route was a useful alternative, particularly when the half-hourly bus failed to turn up. Also, by then, a right-of-way path, albeit still unlit, had been opened up to Woodlands Road, which did not cross any allotments. However, to others in the local community and particularly the elderly or infirm, the Woodlands Road train and subsequent Metrolink stop were a necessity.

The desire to close Woodlands Road largely emanated from the City Council who had plans for two new Metrolink Stops. One of these was to the north of Woodlands Road (in the Bury direction) at Abraham Moss, which is a sports centre-cum-secondary and primary school complex, and perhaps more pertinently lies within the ward represented by the leader of the City Council.

The second was to the south of Woodlands (and in the Central Manchester direction) at Queens Road. Alongside Queens Road was the original Metrolink depot, and there was already a staff-only stop there at which the majority of services already halted.

They argued that these two stops would make Woodlands Road redundant, and in any case, Woodlands Road was "the least used stop on the network" or "one of the least used stops on the network", depending on which of the closure procedures documents one read.

Although the latter was probably true, its usage was not significantly low compared with many other stops, and Transport for Greater Manchester's (TfGM) own figures showed it was used by in excess of a quarter of a million passengers per annum.

They also argued that the users of Woodlands Road would be only marginally inconvenienced by its closure. To prove this, they used the distance between the Woodlands Road and the nearer of the two new stops, Abraham Moss, and the distances between most people's homes and Woodlands Road and Abraham Moss.

However, they used distances as the crow flies, whereas the local street plans meant most Woodlands Road users would have much further to walk and, in many cases passing Woodlands Road to get to Abraham Moss.

Also, the fact that a high proportion of these were the elderly and infirm was totally ignored, as was the lack of nearby bus routes.

Those protesting the closure of Woodlands Road were not averse to the opening of the Queens Road but saw no legitimate case for the effective replacement of Woodlands Road by Abraham Moss and the resultant inconvenience to the former's users. If the latter was convenient for them, as TfGM argued, surely Woodlands Road was equally convenient for potential users of Abraham Moss, so why were the six million pounds construction costs being spent unnecessarily?

Some even saw no reason why Woodlands Road should close even if Abraham Moss opened, given other parts of the Metrolink network had stops just as adjacent. However, TfGM, backed by the City Council were adamant that Woodlands Road had to close. Their closure case was produced by apparently tame consultants who produced a business case for closure overwhelmingly based on the assumption that through passengers would be delayed by some 30 seconds if Woodlands Road remained open.

Based on this assumption, the case argued that a certain number of these through passengers would be deterred from using Metrolink with such negative consequences as increased traffic pollution, etc. The protesters pointed out that a thirty-second delay under normal circumstances would hardly have such dire consequences, but particularly in the case of Metrolink, which does not operate to a timetable but only to a nominal frequency which was rarely adhered to.

Although an intermittent user of Woodlands Road, I had not been immediately aware of the closure threat nor the campaign to save it. In fact, those opposing it had already produced a petition with over 1300 signatures. However, as soon as I became aware of the proposed closure, I obtained copies of the case for closure. As soon as I saw the flaws in the argument for closure, I became an active member of the group fighting it under the banner of Save our Station (SoS). My motivation was that, although the closure would have a relatively minor impact on me personally, I found the case for closure was hardly based on sound facts and statistics and so obviously political that I found it offensive.

The UK 2005 Railways Act required the approval of the Secretary of State for Transport before any station could be closed. The act also required a twelve-week consultation period as part of the closure process.

It was immediately apparent that the timescale proposed by TfGM for the process allowed insufficient time for this consultation period, and one of the first acts of SoS, once constituted, was to point this out, and, as a result, the timescale was extended so that it was compliant with the act. SoS then made sure that good use was made of the consultation period to coordinate and maximise the opposition to the proposed closure.

My own submission consisted of a lengthy document making the case for the station to remain open. Part of this consisted of a survey of the time sequence of trams through the station. This showed that over the survey period, the time interval between trams varied between one and twenty minutes, whereas the advertised frequency was six minutes, thus making a nonsense of the claims about the impact that a thirty-second increase in journey times might have.

Later, I updated my document with the data obtained via freedom of information that over a quarter of a million passengers were using Woodlands Road per annum. Also, I added sample-walking distances between local residences and both Woodlands Roads and Abraham Moss, which showed how nonsensical the closure case's as-the-crow-flies distances were.

Freedom of information was also used to obtain data from Greater Manchester Police showing that the closure case's claims that Woodlands Road was a crime hotspot were also inaccurate.

As well as SoS's involvement in the formal process, it organised several meetings and demonstrations (Rosemary, with her love of baking, supplied refreshments, particularly cakes, for these). The former include one with the director of Metrolink, councillors and other officials, which I chaired. Also, a poster campaign was conducted, which resulted in the majority of the affected residences, well over a thousand, displaying SoS posters. SoS also had its own Facebook page.

All this was accompanied by efforts to involve the media, both local and national, including the specialist railway press. This had limited success, particularly since, although we got radio coverage and I was interviewed several times, the television companies, both BBC and ITV, again ignored the issue.

Interestingly, the Railway Magazine gave the campaign significant coverage, whereas Modern Railways gave it only one brief mention. Surprisingly, given its balanced view on other rail matters, this journal only gives Metrolink positive coverage.

Unfortunately, all our efforts were to no avail. Although the Secretary of State via the Office of the Rail Regulator (ORR) deemed that Woodlands Road could not be closed until both Abraham Moss and Queens Road had opened, immediately when Abraham Moss opened, TfGM cynically reduced the number of trams stopping at Woodlands Road by three quarters, with trams only stopping between 10 am and 4 pm on weekdays.

TfGM's "justification" was that rush hour through passengers could not be delayed. Why this applied to evenings and weekends was never explained, despite the inconsistency being pointed out to TfGM. This situation applied until Queens Road opened, and in the interim, Manchester City Council and TfGM constantly produced passenger numbers for Abraham Moss. Whilst justifying its opening, it did not justify, as they claimed, the closure of Woodland Road and its impact on those who, as a result, stopped using Metrolink or had to walk significantly longer distances to get to it.

Throughout this period, SoS continued its campaign, which included requests for Department of Transport ministers and civil servants as well as ORR officials to visit Woodlands Road so that they could see at first hand the errors and inaccuracies in the closure case. They either declined or ignored the several requests. In contrast, the total closure of Woodlands Road when Queens Road opened was agreed at a meeting at the ORR, which TfGM attended. Surprisingly, a Freedom of Information request for minutes of this meeting produced the response that it had not been minuted.

The third local issue with which I became involved concerned the land opposite 91 Hazelbottom Road. My understanding was that it had been donated to Manchester City Council by a Lord Cawley for the use of the children of the neighbourhood, and indeed, the St Thomas's school football team played there.

During World War II, it was used as the site of one of the anti-aircraft gun batteries protecting Manchester from German air raids, and family folklore has it that I cried when the guns were taken away.

Soon after the war, the City Council sold it to a chemical distribution company who constructed their offices and warehousing on it, and I spent some of my time playing in the half-constructed facility when the builders were not present.

Eventually, the site expanded to be directly opposite number 91. Initially, this was not a problem, but when a planning application was made for the construction of a plant and hard standing for chemical tanks and tankers directly opposite number 91, we naturally objected. Our concerns were not only the eyesore thus created but also the risk to our home and ourselves from the chemicals.

This time we were partially successful in our campaign because although the application was granted and the facilities were built, the company had to build a high earth bank topped with trees to shield us.

Despite this partial success, these issues did not dispel my cynicism about politicians and made me question what improvement devolution of power from central to local government makes, as one is still at the mercy of politicians.

My activist involvement did cover my being asked to involve myself in several community activities. This included being asked by our rector to act as independent chairman of a public meeting concerning the closure of a local church graveyard and the administration of the bodies of those interred there.

The meeting ended with a question and answer session. I directed the questions to who seemed appropriate on the panel of

City Councillors, Clergy and the company that was to handle the task.

After a series of questions handled in this way, one questioner asked if the body of his sister, who had died at the age of six and was buried in the graveyard, could be transferred so that she was reburied alongside their parents.

I felt that the answer was obvious, so I fielded it myself, saying – certainly wherever your parents are currently buried. "Oh," said the questioner, "they are not dead but sat beside me here!"

Stan Price

CHAPTER 28

OUTDOOR PURSUITS PLUS BLUE MOON AND RED ROSE

My life, even before retirement, was not all work. Even though I was never good enough to play sport in any meaningful way, I did indulge in a number of physical or semi-physical activities. One of these was sailing.

I first got involved in dinghy sailing when at Hawker Siddeley. The Woodford works had a sailing club that sailed GP14 dinghies on Errwood Reservoir, which was situated in the Peak District National Park Goyt Valley just to the north of Buxton. The combination of sailing and the beautiful setting was extremely relaxing after a hard day's work, although given the high altitude location, the sailing could be exhilarating, to say the least. Anyway, it enabled me to become reasonably proficient both as a helmsman and a crew.

The club also visited other sailing locations, most notably Lake Windermere and, on one occasion, Loch Lomond in Scotland. Unfortunately, it was the time of the great Scottish midge season, and their attentions made the sailing unpleasant, so we decamped to Fort William and the Sea Loch Linnhe.

My dinghy sailing continued when I joined the CAA, as described in Chapter 12, but I also graduated to larger yachts. These were owned by air traffic controller colleagues and involved several trips across the Channel to France, as well as more local waters.

One scary cross-channel return trip was at night in thick fog. This inevitably meant running on the motor, the noise of which precluded our hearing the sound of large vessels. Given the yacht had no radar and the likelihood of encounters in the Channel, the whole episode was quite scary.

The outward trip had been amusing. We were heading for Cherbourg, but the voyage took far longer than we expected, and we surprisingly arrived at Fécamp, eighty-five miles to the east. The problem turned out to be a beer can left adjacent to the compass.

I also sailed on friends' yachts whilst in the USA, both on the inland waterways and the Atlantic off New Jersey and Florida. In later years I chartered yachts when staying on Kalymnos in Greece. Although by then I had obtained my Yachtmaster Certificate, I still employed a local skipper. One notable trip was from Kalymnos to Patmos in rough weather when I foolishly insisted on staying at the helm for several hours, and in the process, knocked myself out for the next day.

I nearly complemented my yachting certificate by obtaining a private pilot's licence, but this light aircraft flying was only a transient interest, with most of the hours in my logbook being clocked whilst in the USA. There the weather and the cost of hiring a light aircraft was extremely conducive to pursuing the interest. The reverse was true on my return to the UK, and therefore, apart from a few flights, I did not pursue flying as a hobby.

Perhaps this was partially due to another scary incident. Along with a qualified yet inexperienced friend, I was flying in a light aircraft from White Waltham, west of Reading to St Just on the tip of the Cornish peninsula. We got lost in cloud, and when we emerged, we had an argument about where we were. I correctly identified

Marlborough from the main street with the red brick building of Marlborough College at the one end.

After the confusion, we decided to abort the flight at Exeter, where we visited the Cathedral, no doubt to say a prayer for our deliverance. The powered flying actually followed on from some earlier flights in gliders at Woodford whilst I was working there.

Hiking, particularly in the Peak District, was an integral part of my early existence, particularly with the Cubs and Scouts and something I missed when away in London or elsewhere. However, I did do some walking near London as part of my CAA social activities. This took place in the area of Hambleden, northwest of Maidenhead. However pleasant this was, it could not compare with my northern haunts. I resumed walking in them upon my return to Manchester in 1984 under the auspices of the Manchester Pedestrian Club (MPC).

The MPC was reputed to be the world's oldest gentlemen's walking club, and indeed, in 2003, it had its centenary. Its modus operandi was to have two or three walks each Saturday of varying lengths but in the same location. The walks were followed by dinner and drinks at a convivial hostelry.

Apart from a coordinator with the title Walks Convenor, members took it in turn to organise the Saturday and then lead one of the walks. Members wishing to participate in a particular Saturday walk would book in by telephone on the previous Thursday evening. The Saturday walks generally took place in an area that was no more than an hours drive from central Manchester. This meant, to the east and northeast the Pennines, including the West Riding of Yorkshire and the Rossendales, to the south and southeast, the Peak District, North Cheshire and the borders of Staffordshire. The west, given the relatively uninteresting terrain, apart from a seaside walk near Southport and a foray over the border into North Wales, was largely neglected. However, the club had also three weekends away each year organised by that year's president. These could be anywhere in England, Scotland and Wales, and there were even some trips to the continent.

Although not particularly a strong walker, I would participate most weekends and became part of the MPC's inner wheel, so much so that in 1995, I was elected president. This was despite my saying that, given my other commitments, I would not consider myself until I retired. Being the organisational show off I am, instead of three presidential weekends away, I organised four:

> Late March at Padstow in Cornwall travelling by train.
> Late April at Innerleithen in the Scottish Southern Highlands.
> Early June at Burnsall in the Yorkshire Dales.
> Mid October near Keswick in the Lake District.

The latter was a yearly regular, but my objective in the first two was to have two bites at spring walking, given the south/ north separation of the two.

Another of the president's duties was to arrange a Ladies Day whereon the members could invite their wives or partners or other female members of their family. I chose Skipton in Yorkshire with afternoon walks on the moor north of Embsay or around Skipton itself, followed by a buffet dinner on a barge on the nearby Liverpool to Leeds canal.

Prior to becoming president, I held within the club the position of "Writer of Retrospect". Retrospect was a chronicle of the club's activities on a yearly basis, and it was included in the club's yearbook after being read out at the Annual General Meeting held before Christmas. I wrote Retrospect for several years, and although I kept it factually accurate insofar as the walks, meals and weather, etc, were concerned, I did spice it with some whimsical humour, which seemed to go down very well with the members.

I also often had to propose an after-dinner vote of thanks to whoever had arranged the walks or weekend. One such occasion was at Capel Curig in North Wales. To quote the Retrospect writer of that year, not me - "the vote of thanks was proposed by Stan Price speaking, as it appeared, in fluent and eloquent Welsh. He later admitted it was fluent and eloquent gibberish, concocted from Welsh station names".

An MPC party at the Cross Keys Inn in Saddleworth.

I found the MPC to be a delightful organisation and an oasis in a world full of bureaucracy and where old-style courtesy was in short supply. It, however, eventually succumbed to the world outside with instead of, for example, quarterly committee meetings, lasting less than half an hour, the governance became a series of debates about rules and finance.

The fellowship also declined, and I was the only member of the club to attend the funeral of a long-standing member, who, although having returned to his native Edinburgh, always made an effort to participate in the club's activities. He even attended the Cornwall weekend I organised when president.

Membership of the MPC also had several spin-off benefits, including significantly enlarging my knowledge of the northwest of England's countryside and its hostelries. More importantly, several of its members became long-standing friends. My resigning from the club after over twenty years of membership came about because of a dispute between one of them and the club.

This member and friend always walked with his two dogs, and many members were concerned that he did not keep them on the lead sufficiently. It was a concern with which I had some sympathy.

Nevertheless, the club appointed him president and writer of Retrospect and therefore condoned it for a number of years.

However, my friend had a very bohemian personality, which irked some of the smaller minded members. They therefore contrived to use the freedom he allowed his dogs on walks to pursue a vendetta against him. To me, this vendetta was a much more important concern than the dog issue.

Nevertheless, the then powers-that-be in the Club failed to separate the two issues, and I felt I no longer wanted to be part of an organisation that condoned such vendettas.

Notwithstanding the unhappy ending of membership of the MPC, it gave me many outstanding memories over the twenty years I was a member. One or two were less than pleasant because of the weather and/or the conditions, most notably returning from the Tan Hill Inn, the highest pub in England in absolutely atrocious wind and rain. It was the only occasion I experienced the desire just to lie down on the open moor and let fate take over.

Many of the best moments were in the warmth and security of the pub after a winter walk, particularly before the open fire of the Lantern Pike Inn, Little Hayfield, Derbyshire, on what was normally the last walk before Christmas. Other memories were on the actual walks, an example being waving the yellow flag to summon the River Camel ferry to take the party back from Rock to Padstow on the Cornish weekend referred to above. Incidentally, this walk included one of my favourite locations – St Enodoc's Church, where the poet John Betjeman is buried. The Saxon church itself had been buried in the sand dunes for several centuries. The tranquillity of the spot was remarkable, with the only sound being the distant booming of the surf on the Doom sandbar where the Camel met the sea.

As indicated in Chapter 1, since an early age, I had been an ardent supporter of Manchester City Football Club, and prior to regular Saturday walking with the MPC, I was a frequent attendee, along with my brother, at Manchester City matches. I did this even when living in London. The switch from regular spectator at football matches to walker was not just because of a change of interest on my part. I still follow the fortunes of Manchester City passionately. A significant factor was the behaviour of football crowds, and the disasters of Hillsborough and Heysel came as no surprise to me.

Manchester City, during my time following them, suffered from extremely erratic bouts of success and failure. During the 1950s, they were relatively successful but then went into decline, culminating in their relegation from the first division of English Soccer in the 1962/63 season. One of their defining results in this was a 1-6 away loss to West Ham, and I had the misfortune, on leaving the ground, of bumping into an old schoolmate who was a supporter of Manchester United.

Towards the end of that decade, City's fortunes revived, and they went on to win the First Division Championship and European Cup

Winners Cup, as well as two other cups. I attended the European final in Vienna and also the final match at Newcastle of their 1968 championship-winning season.

The title was between City and United, and the joy of City's winning at Newcastle was compounded by Sunderland beating United in Manchester. I recall us meeting Sunderland supporters in Leeds as we crossed on our respective route's home. However, what ensued became just an alcoholic blur.

City declined again in the 1990s and actually fell into the third division for a season. They got promoted back to the second division via the playoffs in 1999, having finished third. By then, I was no longer an active spectator and was, in fact, watching a Cricket World Cup game between the West Indies and Australia at Old Trafford. With two or three minutes to play, we learnt that City's opponents, Gillingham, were winning 2 – 0. To my great relief, City scored twice then to take the game to extra time, subsequently winning on penalties.

Since then, to my tribal delight, they have gone on to become one of the best club sides in the world, and I deem it reasonable compensation for the times I slunk away from grounds such a Shrewsbury and Halifax after a defeat.

Cricket was my other great sporting interest. However, unlike football, where although not disinterested in the England side, I did not follow it fanatically, I followed both Lancashire and England cricket as a spectator wherever possible.

My support for England culminated in 2010 after my retirement when Rosemary and I went to Australia to take in two of the Ashes test matches in Brisbane and Adelaide. I was lucky in that the series was one of the few where England performed creditably and won the series with a draw in Brisbane (England were 517 for one wicket with Alistair Cook 235 not out) and a win in Adelaide.

I would also watch all five days of England's home matches at Old Trafford in Manchester, plus days at their matches in London, Birmingham and Nottingham. Particularly at Old Trafford, I witnessed some of the great cricket moments, including, as described in Chapter 1, all of Laker's nineteen wickets against Australia and in later years Shane Warne's ball of the century that bowled Mike Gatting.

Upon my return to Manchester, I became a member and later a Life Member at Old Trafford. This facilitated my taking in segments of Lancashire's county matches, even when I was still working. I also attended most of their one-day finals at Lords.

The only time they have won the championship outright in my lifetime was in 2011. They won it on the final day of the final match of the season. Unfortunately, I had foolishly arranged to be on holiday at the time and only learnt of it via an Internet café in Rome, bemusing the local Italian attendees with my whoops of delight.

Rosemary was also a cricket fan and a member of Lancashire, attending most of the matches with me. This included all the five days of the test matches at Old Trafford in Manchester, where our both being members meant we could obtain at least six tickets. We therefore invited a number of friends, and Rosemary again catered splendidly, and we also dined out en masse most evenings at different upmarket restaurants. Our regular guests included my doctor and friend Bhishma and his friend Ashok, another medic. Ashok was a member of Warwickshire, and he kindly reciprocated our hospitality with tickets for international matches at Edgbaston, Birmingham.

Old Trafford cricket ground was the scene of two embarrassing encounters. One day during the 2005 Ashes match between England and Australia, a young woman and baby sat in seats in front of us. I chuntered to Rosemary about the "stupidity" of bringing a baby to a cricket match only to discover it was the wife and child of Andrew Flintoff, the star player of the series.

On another occasion, after lunch in the County restaurant, Rosemary and I took our seats to watch the cricket. One of Lancashire's bowlers was being hit all over by the opposition batsmen, and again I chuntered. To my amazement, a spectator nearby took umbrage and said he was fed up with my comments complaining I had been going on for hours. When I pointed out that this was not possible as I had just come from the restaurant, he became even more offensive, saying that a person of my girth could not know anything about cricket. Eventually, several other spectators calmed him down. He claimed he was the father of the Lancashire captain, who had the responsibility of choosing who should bowl. Incidentally, the bowler concerned, James Anderson, became one of the greatest bowlers in the world, but in defence of my observations, it was while he was going through a well-documented bad spell.

CHAPTER 29

GREECE, PARTICULARLY KALYMNOS

As a student, I saw the movie "*A Summer Holiday*" at the Odeon in Camberwell Green. In the movie, the characters played by Cliff Richard and his backing group, The Shadows, travel from London to Athens on a red double-decker London bus. Friends and I decided to emulate these characters and travelled overland to Athens. From then on, Greece became my holiday destination of choice.

Early trips stopped short at Athens. One of these early trips was by rail partly on a through train from Cologne to Athens, with a different restaurant car being attached to the train in each country we traversed. This included Yugoslavia, where the abiding memory was the aggressiveness of the border guards and particularly, for understandable reasons, to German passengers.

Athens soon became passé, so I soon took to travelling on from Athens to the islands, particularly Paros and Mykonos in the Cyclades. These trips generally involved overnight flights to Athens followed by a workmen's bus down to the port of Piraeus, where one caught the ferry to the Aegean islands. Incidentally, if one travelled on the bus before 8 am, it was free.

On two occasions I was accompanied: once by Uncle Ted's grandson, Tony Trott and once by my New Zealand mate, Steve Smith.

Often I went solo and, on one occasion, went as far as Crete, but this time by air from Athens in a propeller-driven Douglas DC6B. At the time, there were no direct flights to Crete from the UK. I stayed at the then only pension in Malia bay, where the muzak constantly played Charles Aznavour's "Yesterday When I Was Young".

Another of these trips was to the island of Andros, but this time taking the ferry from the port of Rafina. The holiday was, in retrospect, tinged with tragedy because soon after, the ferry I travelled on sank with significant loss of life. I remember at the time thinking the vessel was somewhat top-heavy. Also, it was just before the death of my father. Perhaps as an omen, the weather on Andros was unsettled, and I still recall the constant wind whistling mournfully through the pines.

Another Greek holiday was a villa one at Agios Nikolaos on Crete. The holiday company had made an error in the bookings, and instead of the villa being occupied equally between males and females, I found myself sharing it with a dozen attractive girls and one other guy. Furthermore, this guy was rather inept, being unable to swim or sunbathe, for example, and blunder prone – he even lost the keys to his luggage. This did not endear him to the girls, so I had to shoulder the male role essentially alone, which turned out to be rather demanding.

Later, I took my brother John on another Greek holiday, flying to Athens. From there, we took a ferry to Paros and then another to Santorini. Here, the mode of travel from where the ferries berthed up to the town was still on the back of one of a train of donkeys. This was quite scary given that the steps were slippery from the dung from the countless donkeys, and there was nothing to prevent one from falling hundreds of feet back to the sea!

From Santorini, we took another ferry onto Heraklion in Crete, where we hired a jeep. This resulted in an incident when we tried to follow a road along the south-eastern shore of Crete that was clearly marked on the map. On the ground, however, the road petered out and became a boulder-strewn track. By a miracle, we managed to negotiate this until we came to a village that was on a regular road. Our vehicular approach to the village was so unusual we had to move the chairs and tables of two tavernas before we were able to proceed into the village.

The visit to Crete concluded with our taking the overnight ferry to Piraeus in a storm of such violence I thought it was prudent to wake my brother, who was sleeping through it.

The next time I followed the Paros/Santorini/Crete itinerary was on my first holiday with Rosemary, introducing her to Greek Island hopping. By then, the donkeys of Santorini had been replaced with more salubrious transport, and Malia Bay on Crete, instead of comprising a single pension, had regrettably become a full-blown typical Mediterranean holiday resort. However, whilst on Crete, we hiked down the Samaria Gorge and walked around the World War II Malmae battle site.

We had two or three further holidays on Crete, including one where the weather was so bad that there was considerable flooding. Then we decided that we would like a change. I was at the time carrying out the assignment for Vernon's in Liverpool, and by chance, their office complex included a travel agency.

Up to then, I had sorted out my own holidays, but being rather busy at the time, I asked the agency to sort me out a remote Greek Island venue. However, we were appalled to find the place they had chosen was Kardamena on Kos. At the time, Kardamena was a fishing village, being grossly overdeveloped for the tourist trade with all the building that involved and not what we required. However, whilst there we did take a day trip to Kalymnos, the island immediately to the north of Kos, little knowing that in several respects it would effectively become a second home.

The return flight became a saga in its own right. It was scheduled for lunchtime on a baking hot day, and as the aircraft was an early Boeing 737, I thought it highly likely it would not be able to take off with sufficient fuel to get to Manchester without refuelling. Some other passengers, on overhearing me, were quite outspoken in saying I was talking nonsense, but I was vindicated when soon after take-off, the pilot announced we would indeed have to stop to refuel.

This took place expeditiously at Rotterdam, with the passengers staying on board, but our take-off run was aborted when a tyre blew out. The subsequent delay meant the pilots would be out of hours, so we had to spend the night in Rotterdam. Again this was expeditiously handled, and we were put up in a four-star hotel preceded by a reasonable dinner. Although the ongoing flight to Manchester was scheduled for fairly early the next morning, this would still prevent me from making a business meeting in Edinburgh that I had unwisely scheduled for that day. So I took a cab at first light back to Rotterdam Airport and boarded a City Hopper to Heathrow and the shuttle up to Edinburgh, arriving in time for my meeting.

I nearly did not make it for UK Air Traffic Control had computer problems. These were quickly resolved, possibly because of a phone call I made to my contacts.

My return to Manchester that evening was by train from Edinburgh.

Meanwhile, I had gallantly left Rosemary in Rotterdam with two lots of luggage, including duty frees. UK customs accepted her explanation without penalty, and a male couple assisted her with her two lots of baggage. The couple were of assistance in another way in that they recommended a hotel on the west side of Kalymnos where they had been staying.

The following year we decided to give their recommendation a try and made a booking at the hotel. However, we were later advised a bar was being built on the roof, and it would be noisy. So we therefore switched to an adjacent hotel. Kalymnos, not then having an airport, we flew again to Kos and then took a taxi to the local port of Mastichari from where the ferry with the shortest sea journey to Kalymnos operated.

After a few days, we chartered a yacht with a skipper for the day, and he took us to Vathi on the east side of Kalymnos facing Turkey. Vathi lies at the head of a rocky fiord, and as we entered the fiord, we encountered a square-rigged tall ship setting sail. The sight of this beautiful vessel with the cliffs in the background and the uniformed crew manning the yards was a sight to behold.

Later in the holiday, we visited Vathi for the second time, but this time by foot. The fiord is complemented by an inlet on the west side, and there is a spectacular albeit rough walk between the two, although now a little-used road connects the two. Despite leaving rather late and getting caught in the heat of the day, we successfully completed the walk, returning to the west side of the island and our hotel by bus.

Later still in the holiday, we booked a taxi guide to take us round more of the island. This turned out to be Manolis Kolettis, who owned a pension in Vathi. Manolis made it one of the stops on his tour, where he offered us refreshments. His pension was above Reina, the village where the fiord ends and Vathi (Valley) begins. Unusually for a Greek island, Vathi has underground water, and as a result, it is cultivated and very green. The pension, therefore, has spectacular views in both directions. One way looks down the fiord and over the blue sea to Turkey, and in the other direction up the green valley with spectacular mountains on each side. I was immediately smitten with the beauty of the place and the tranquillity. So we decided our next holiday would be in Vathi staying with Manolis, and so it transpired.

Vathi Looking East down the "fiord" to Turkey.

While staying with Manolis, we chartered a yacht, and it is possible that the resultant exposure to the sun made Rosemary very dehydrated, plus she caught a bug. Her condition deteriorated, and she became very cold and was shaking, so Manolis drove us to a doctor in the main town, Pothia.

The doctor immediately decided she should be admitted to hospital, where she spent four days. The conditions were rather primitive, with the ward infested with cockroaches and the like, while the food was abysmal. The expectation was that friends and relatives would provide the non-medical care.

By the time Rosemary had sufficiently recovered to fly home, we had missed our flight to Manchester. The airline could only offer us standby on a flight to London Gatwick. Unfortunately, this was scheduled for the middle of the night, and Rosemary was in no fit condition to spend the hours between the last ferry's arrival in Kos and take off time at Kos Airport. I therefore checked us into a hotel at Mastichari and booked a taxi from there to take us to the airport at approximately 2 am.

However, the taxi did not turn up, and we were left in a completely deserted and pitch black Mastichari, wondering desperately what to do. Then, out of the darkness emerged a lit up charter coach taking Dutch tourists to the port. I chased after it and explained to the driver and courier our situation, and they kindly took us to the airport once they had disembarked their passengers.

Fortunately, we got on the flight and arrived at Gatwick early on a Sunday morning. Unfortunately, we could not get onto a flight up to Manchester, so took the train up to London Victoria, from whence we got a taxi to Euston. On boarding the Manchester train from there, Rosemary, as a relief from the Greek Hospital food, immediately ordered two large bacon sandwiches from the buffet.

Undeterred by this experience, we returned to Kalymnos the following and subsequent years, which I think endeared us to the locals. One of these visits coincided with Rosemary's cousin's planned wedding to a Greek guy. The event was to be in Arta on the western Greek mainland, and the plan was for us to break off for a week from a holiday on Kalymnos to attend the wedding.

We therefore took the ferry to Piraeus, where I picked up a hire car to travel the approximately 300 kilometres to Arta. Manolis had strongly advised me not to drive, and he was vindicated when I missed the turning to the west for Corinth, and we found ourselves lost in the centre of Athens. We ended up calling in at a doctor's surgery to ask the way, the doctor being the only local who could speak English.

Eventually, we arrived at the hotel in Arta only to be met on the steps by Rosemary's six foot two tall ex-Coldstream Guardsman father holding up his hands saying, "Go back, its orf". It was indeed off, the Greek groom having done a runner. We therefore spent the week consoling the would-be bride and driving the other guests around, including Rosemary's father, who had flown direct from the UK.

Having had trouble positioning the car on the ferry across the Gulf of Corinth on the outward journey, I took a route on the return journey along the northern shore of the Gulf. Although this route was extremely picturesque, navigation was again a problem, and the journey took much longer than anticipated. Nevertheless, we arrive in Piraeus just in time for our booked ferry back to Kalymnos, and soon after boarding, I lapsed exhausted into a deep sleep in our cabin.

These early trips to Kalymnos involved flying from Manchester to Kos and then taking the ferry via Mastichari to Kalymnos. However, with my interest in railways, I then began to research how one might travel by train from Manchester to Kalymnos, and this became our mode of travel for a number of years.

Unlike the time of my first trip to Athens by rail, the war that followed the break up of Yugoslavia was happening, so that route was no longer available. What became our normal route was from the UK to the Italian Adriatic ports of Ancona, Bari and on one occasion Trieste then by ferry to Patras in Greece. Patras at times exhibited the sad sight of hundreds of Albanian refugees trying to stow away on the ferries.

We usually came back direct, typically taking seventy hours from sitting on Manolis' terrace to entering our Manchester home with two nights sleeping on ferries and one on a sleeper train from Italy.

As recounted in Chapter 30, the outward and return rail trips from the UK to these ports was, with the few exceptions, relatively straightforward. Getting to and from Patras to Piraeus for the ferry to Kalymnos was fraught with problems. Theoretically, it should have been easy as there was a direct service on the narrow gauge railway line from Patras to Piraeus through Athens. However, even before this line was disrupted for a variety of reasons using the train for this segment of our overall journey was normally impractical.

In fact, we only used it twice. The first time was on our first overland rail trip. We boarded our scheduled train at Patras to find it was a slow one consisting of antiquated coaches with no air conditioning pulled by an equally antiquated diesel. As we proceeded east, the train fell behind even its slow schedule, and it was apparent that the diesel was ailing. The journey was so extended that a number of Greek ladies gathered around us to admire Rosemary's intricate knitting.

Despite the addition of a second diesel, the whole train ground to a halt in the mountains in the dark, some way short of Athens. We therefore followed the example of the locals and decamped onto the tracks; we were in a loop but not in a station. After a while, the locals flagged down the following train, and we boarded it. Fortunately, it was Piraeus bound, and we were booked into a hotel there overnight, so our lateness meant we did not miss a ferry connection.

The only other occasion we took the train it was much more successful but in the reverse direction. It was a diesel multiple unit express with air conditioning and first-class. Furthermore, we discovered that we could check our luggage in the left luggage at Piraeus and collect it at the left luggage in Patras.

There was, however, a more, but not completely, reliable alternative. The ferry company ran a connecting coach service between Patras and Piraeus, and that was what we eventually took to using. However, on one occasion, on the return trip, the ferry from Kalymnos was so late we missed the coach, and on another occasion, it simply failed to turn up, thus putting our connections across Europe in jeopardy. On both occasions, we had no other recourse than to take a taxi for the two hundred plus kilometre journey just catching our Italy bound ferry at Patras in the nick of time.

After our final trip to Greece by rail, which resulted in the incident with the Americans in the Athens Airport Hotel and our subsequent, direct flight from Athens to Kalymnos, we reverted to flying the whole way, or at least to Kos. Incidentally, the airport on Kalymnos opened while we were there. It was constructed by filling in the gap between two adjacent mountains, with the result it was susceptible to closure in all but the lightest winds and was only suitable for aircraft carrying up to twenty passengers.

Whatever our mode of travel, and apart from the yacht chartering, our routine in Vathi generally settled into rising late and going for breakfast at the hotel across the square in Reina followed by a pre-lunch swim. After a siesta, the evening was spent dining at one of the tavernas. We had to be careful because of the rivalry between some of the tavernas, and we returned one year to find one taverna had been deliberately dynamited.

On a happier note, one of the most memorable evenings was an impromptu sing-along at one of the tavernas with a dozen nationalities involved.

Other memorable events within Vathi were the barbeques at the pension and on adjacent beaches arranged by Manolis for his guests. He also provided the transport to the latter in his motorboat. There were also dinner parties at the home of ex-pats Sarah and Mike, who lived up the valley, plus drinks sessions at the home of Anna and Michaelis. He was a retired tanker skipper who had built a bungalow at a stunning location on the walls of the fiord above the height of the yacht's masts moored in the fiord.

Vathi was not only scenically beautiful but extremely tranquil most of the time, the only sounds being the natural ones of goat bells, donkey brays and cockerel crows, albeit the last in the hours of the morning. The only normal times it was less than tranquil was around noon when tourist boats from Kos and the other touristy western side of Kalymnos disgorged their passengers for an hour or so. The loss of tranquillity was offset by the entertainment the tourists' antics provided.

The other exceptional times when the tranquillity was disturbed was when there were tensions between Greece and Turkey, and fighter jets were flying overhead and warships moored in the fiord.

On our early visits to Vathi, we would visit this westerly side for dinner, particularly the island of Telendos, which because of its shape, also reminded me of Navarone in the Alistair MacLean novels. During later visits, the only repeated excursions from Vathi we undertook were into the main town, Pothia, to visit the bank. I also took the opportunity to buy the English newspapers, which was a mistake because the contents, plus the bustle of the bowl that is Pothia, impacted negatively my feeling of tranquillity that Vathi had induced.

Also, during our final visits, a road had been built funded by the European Commission from Vathi direct to the northwest coast, and on a couple of occasions, friends took us over this spectacular route. Interestingly, it seemed little used.

Our holidays in Vathi, with one exception when we went in May, were taken in late summer. My logic was that this then prepared us for the English winter. However, whenever they were taken, they provided me with a respite from my normal, particularly busy work schedule. To this end, even in the days of mobile phones, I made little contact with home, apart from when there were concerns about the health of my mother.

Stan Price

CHAPTER 30

THE ARTS, TRAINS (AGAIN) AND CATS

Apart from reading during my formative years, despite the influence of my mother, I was not significantly exposed to any wider cultural or cerebral interests. However, this changed as I matured. Perhaps this maturation would have happened faster if I had taken the arts rather than the sciences route at secondary school. That said, I still had to study English literature, which introduced me to the works of Shakespeare, for example, although at the time, I regarded it as a chore rather than enlightenment. My lack of a broader-based education, both formal and informal, was probably the reason I failed GCE A-level General Studies.

My maturation is perhaps illustrated by the changes in the newspapers I read. As a child, I read the Express, which my parents read, and later I moved on, firstly to the Telegraph and then the Times. The latter move was perhaps more a function of increasing the challenge of the respective crosswords than anything else. It culminated in my becoming an aficionado of the weekly Times prize crossword, which I can generally accomplish with minimal input from the dictionary and thesaurus. However, this takes me a matter of hours and days rather than the minutes of geniuses. Also, after they hit the western world, I became addicted to sudokus.

I did have a brief flirtation with the Guardian newspaper and even during my time in the States had it airmailed out to me. However, I became disillusioned with its reporting of the goings-on in Washington, especially Watergate, which did not align with what I was experiencing, and decided it could be relied on less than the press generally.

As indicated in earlier chapters, I developed an early interest in classical music, and as well as the encounter with the work of Elgar on the radio, I was taken on a school trip to listen to Manchester's Hallé orchestra. The concert was conducted by the legendary Sir John Barbirolli in the King's Hall of Belle Vue Pleasure Gardens. The unlikely venue was because the Hallé's regular home, the Free Trade Hall, was being rebuilt, having been heavily damaged in the World War II German Blitz on Manchester.

Given my interest in classical music, my parents furnished me with a record player when I went up to University. Immediately, I purchased a number of records, the first being a recording of Holst's *The Planets Suite*.

Upon my return to Manchester in 1982, I became, along with Rosemary, a season ticket holder at the Hallés Opus series concerts, as well as other selective ones of the Hallé and the Manchester-based BBC Philharmonic.

My concert-going was not, however, just restricted to Manchester. I was an intermittent concertgoer during my years in London and the USA, and during my years with the Met Police, I attended the BBC lunchtime concerts at St John's in Smith Square. There were also notable concert attendances in the Opera House, Sydney, during my 2010 visit to Australia, in Ravello Italy at the Festival and a magical night time open-air concert on the Greek Island of Paros.

Apart from my drumming in the Boy Scouts and a transient semi-singing stand, Rex Harrison style, in a sleazy club in Indianapolis, I could not claim any musical talent myself. Many around me could and were associated with Oldham Choral Society, and therefore, to assist them, I acted as its promotions manager for a limited time after my 1984 return to Manchester.

My interest in music was not just confined to the classical genre. Until the 1980s, I listened to whatever the mainstream popular music of the day was. After then I lost interest and used this to wind up younger people in the record industry who had adjoining offices to PPSL by saying, "there has not been any good pop music since Buddy Holly died".

In this, I was partially a hypocrite because, in the 1960s and 70s, I was especially a fan of soul music and especially The Sound of Philadelphia (TSOP). This included well-known acts such as Harold Melvin and the Blue Notes; The O'Jays; Teddy Pendergrass; Billy Paul, and lesser-known ones such as Archie Bell and the Drells. Some of these songs such as, "*Me and Mrs Jones*", still haunt me in a melancholic way to this day.

Unlike my interest in classical music, I did not attend pop concerts or festivals but listened to the radio, television and records and tapes. The latter included the utilisation of a bulky 8-track player in my MGB car.

I also was a fan of light music, particularly the score of musicals, with West Side Story being my especial favourite. I got to know all the words and once was nearly thrown out of the Minskoff Theatre on Broadway as a result of Japanese tourists complaining about my singing along with the cast.

This love of musicals must have been partly inherited from my parents, who had been regular attendees prior to World War II. It, therefore, gave me immense pleasure in their later years to take them to the opening night of "*Evita*" in the West End despite an altercation between my dad and one of the theatre knights in the interval bar.

It was also de rigueur in my student years to be interested in jazz, but despite many evenings at hops and in west end clubs, including the Marquee, I never became a fan. I used to find it ironic that such a free format art form should have its rituals, including a drum solo in the middle of every number. This was accompanied by a break in the dancing while everyone stood around and applauded wildly at the end, irrespective of the quality of the solo. Other forms of music such as acid rock and punk largely left me cold.

Apart from musicals, I intermittently attended the theatre, starting as a child with pantomime, particularly at the Queens Park Hippodrome in North Manchester. This was one of the innumerable local theatres that closed partly because of the advent of television.

My attendances at theatres in the West End included "*Son of Oblamov*" and "*The Bed Sitting Room*". starring Spike Milligan. The plot of the latter concerned Spike being atomised and transformed into a bed sitting room after a nuclear war, which under a Labour government had been the shortest World War on record.

My attendance at the former was somewhat embarrassing as my girlfriend and I entered our seats in the fourth or fifth row of the stalls after the performance had started. Detecting our movement, Spike advanced to the front of the stage and called for the house lights. He then pointed at us and declaimed, "the story so far."

I also had an active role of sorts in the theatre during my student years and my time as an apprentice at Hawker Siddeley. This included scriptwriting, producing and acting in satirical reviews. The latter enjoyed some success, but it never occurred to me to take my involvement any further.

One of the sketches I wrote for the Hawker Siddeley Apprentice Christmas Party involved me auditioning for attractive girls.

This took place in an office I had been allocated in the middle of the shop floor at the Chadderton Factory. One day, two senior foremen sheepishly knocked on the door and said the workforce was most curious at what I did, given the constant stream of girls visiting the office. "Sorry," I said, "but it is Air Ministry confidential," and at that, they withdrew.

Until my 1984 return to Manchester, I was also a regular filmgoer. This started in childhood with an early memory being of seeing "the Cruel Sea" in black and white. I had been given an unabridged copy of the book when I was ten. It had a significant influence on me, with the wren heroine, Julie Hallam, becoming my idea of an ideal woman.

Later film memories include attending the New York opening of "*The Way We Were*", starring Barbara Streisand and Robert Redford. Almost inevitably, I have watched a lot of television, particularly sport, upmarket quizzes and crime dramas. Sadly though, a lot of the time, the television has to me been simply moving wallpaper while I indulged in something else.

My general knowledge was furthered by my interest in railways. Apart from the obvious way it improved my knowledge of geography, the naming of locomotives added to my historical know-how on such matters as the names of royalty, military figures and even exotic species of animals and plants. It also introduced me to management techniques such as rostering.

I was not only interested in railways as a trainspotter in my formative years or as a means of providing me with business travel. Apart from a gap around the mid-1960s, which unfortunately coincided with the demise of steam locomotives in the UK, railways fascinated me both as an established and developing industry and historically, partly as nostalgia for my train spotting days.

My interest in the contemporary railway took the form of following developments in services, routes, infrastructure, and rolling stock. I also was fascinated but often depressed by the interaction between railways and politicians. This interest took the form of regular subscriptions to the magazines Modern Railways and the Railway Magazine, use of the internet, coupled with occasional trips to travel on lines and trains that were new or that I had not travelled on before. I was also, for some time, a member of the Railway Study Association until its demise.

My nostalgia interest took the form of subscriptions to three magazines dealing with the past as well as the Railway Magazine. I also travelled on heritage lines, most notably the East Lancashire Railway and also travelled on steam locomotive hauled trips on the UK mainline. The latter I coupled with fine dining. The most notable of these was a two-day trip from London to Glasgow and Edinburgh and back to London. This started early on a Saturday morning, and poor planning on my part meant a friend kindly driving Rosemary and me down from Manchester to London only to get the special train back north.

The return journey on the Sunday had a major delay through low water pressure at Edinburgh Waverley, so that the watering of the loco took far longer than planned. The delay was not totally wasted for me as it enabled, along with the Edinburgh member of the Manchester Pedestrian Club referred to in the previous chapter, me to demolish a bottle of Talisker single malt whisky.

Rosemary had planned to leave the train at York to travel back to Manchester, but because of the late-running, alighted at Berwick-upon-Tweed and took regular service trains. I carried on to London, this time having had the foresight to arrange a business meeting there on the Monday. The train was so delayed I arrived there hours late at 2 pm. By then, the restaurant cars supplies were much diminished, so the catering during the final hours was reduced to bacon butties swilled down with Châteauneuf-du-Pape.

Another memorable UK train trip resulted from the sheer amount of train travel I had clocked up on business. I was a member of the British Railways Frequent Traveller Club. Upon privatisation, this was wound up, and, as a consolation, members were offered two first-class weekend returns for two. One was used visiting Rosemary's middle daughter, Karen, in Cromer. For the second, I thought about what was the maximum use I could make of it. I decided upon Thurso in the extreme north of Scotland. We therefore travelled on a Friday over to York from where we took the Flying Scotsman Express to Aberdeen. From there, we took a train to Inverness. The next day we travelled up and down to Thurso. Finally, on the Sunday, we took the Inverness to London Highland Chieftain Express back to York, thence home.

My special train trips were not confined to the UK. Two of them were in New Zealand's South Island - the Taieri Gorge Railway from Dunedin return and the TranzAlpine from Greymouth to Christchurch over the Southern Alps. My sixtieth birthday treat was the ultimate train trip, the Orient Express from Venice to London. It formed part of our return journey from our annual stay on Kalymnos, the other part being the ferry from Greece to Trieste and then the train to Venice. The Orient Express lived up to its reputation, with black-tie dinner and cocktails in the piano bar being the highlight. We arrived at London Victoria dead on time, but then problems began.

Blockages on the lines north from Euston and St Pancras meant our shuttling with copious amounts of luggage between the two until we got a late train to Sheffield. There the promised connection to Manchester turned out to be by coach, and to insult to injury, the driver did not know his way into Manchester, and I had to direct him.

Living it up.

However, this did not detract from our time on the Orient Express, but other vacation European train journeys were less salubrious. This particularly applied to our last rail trip to Greece in 2014. For this trip we, travelled via Cologne, where we boarded the night sleeper to Vienna, our stopping off point en-route. Immediately, the steward told us that the restaurant car had broken down in Amsterdam, and all he had for us to eat was a single sandwich. What was most galling was we would have had time to dine in Cologne if only we had known.

Things did not improve in Vienna; the weather being bitterly cold for the three days we were there, and we only had summer clothing. The restaurant car on the Bucharest to Athens sleeper when we continued our onward journey was reasonable, but amazingly, apart from the railway staff, we were the only diners.

We alighted from the sleeper in Thessalonica at 5 am to catch a faster overtaking train to Athens, which was necessary in order to catch our flight from Athens to Kalymnos. However, although we had tickets, we were not allowed to board the fast train without reservations. It had not been possible to obtain these in the UK. In order to make our Kalymnos flight from Athens, after some rapid improvisation, we took a six-hour coach journey.

Unfortunately, we missed the flight by ten minutes. But Olympic airlines booked us on the flight the next day. Being extremely tired and dirty, we checked into the airport hotel. Refreshed, we went for dinner in the hotel, and I, somewhat understandably, overindulged. Unfortunately, this led to me haranguing three Americans at the next table with all that was wrong with the USA, from their president to black soul clubs in Philadelphia. The lady of the trio was particularly offended, so I felt obliged to leave a note of apology with reception when we checked out the next day.

The previous rail trips to Kalymnos all involved at least one stopover on the outward journey. Two of these were in Venice, including the year when we returned on the Orient Express, as recounted previously. Other Italian venues included Milan and Rome. Apart from the Cologne Vienna trip, the only other time when we did not journey via Paris was when we stopped over in Luxembourg, including dinner with an old University friend and his wife. This was the occasion when on the return journey I chaired the European Commission Workshop in Brussels.

Otherwise, our route was Eurostar to Paris and then the TGV to stopovers which included Marseille and Lausanne. The ongoing routes from these include along the Côte d'Azur in the case of the former, and through the Alps, including Mont Blanc in the case of the latter. This was on a beautiful Sunday morning when we were the only occupants of a first-class carriage. During this Lausanne stopover, we had taken the sail around Lake Geneva.

Journeys to and from Greece were not the only occasions we took continental rail journeys via Paris. We had several visits to friends who had a summer home at Brignoles in Provence taking the TGV to Aix-en-Provence. Also, we travelled to and from Naples and Salerno for holidays on Italy's Amalfi Coast.

Train travel in Italy was generally a pleasant experience, particularly running down the Adriatic coast from Milan or Bologna to Ancona or Bari sampling pasta and Frascati in the restaurant cars. Interestingly, for a time, these were operated by the English company – The Little Chef.

Generally, connections were met, albeit at times with some nervousness on my part. This was none more so than when we had a connection at five in the morning in Verona off the Paris to Venice sleeper. After leaving Paris, it was announced it would not be stopping at Verona. In the event it did, and we made our ongoing connection to Bologna with seven minutes to spare.

On one return trip on the Rome to Paris sleeper, we were awakened in the early hours of the morning to find our coach was the only vehicle in a vast station. Our principal concern was, "where was the rest of our train?" There were no staff to enlighten us, apart from a non-English speaking wheel tapper and shunter. It was with much relief to us that, after half an hour, the rest of our train emerged, backing from the darkness, and the shunter attached us to the rear and off we went.

Apparently, what had happened was that our coach, which had started in the middle of the train, had developed an electrical fault. This had affected the following coaches, so the decision had been taken to detach our coach and attach it to the rear. We subsequently found out the station was Turin Porta Nuova.

Unfortunately, as the years went on, the quality of European sleeper travel deteriorated, culminating in a horrendous experience on the Rome to Paris sleeper in 2013. Even our complaints were appallingly handled by the operator, Abellio.

In contrast, we never had any bad experiences on Eurostar between London and Paris although on one occasion because of a French railway strike we had to revert, at forty-eight hours notice, to a Stanstead to Naples flight. The Paris southerly terminus for all these trips was the Gare de Lyon with its remarkable Blue Train Restaurant, which we sampled during one of our overnight stays in Paris.

I also expressed my nostalgia for my train spotting days through model railways. My aim was to create a layout based on the height of my train spotting years, 1957, before the large-scale advent of diesels on the UK lines that was authentic to the South Lancashire scene that I had known. To that end, I acquired a number of locomotives, carriages, trucks and track work in OO gauge. I started by laying out a prototype track structure on four large boards, which could be accommodated on the dining room table at 91 Hazelbottom. This was set up for the week after Christmas for a number of years whilst we had meals on trays in the sitting room.

Then I made a big mistake. Upon my retirement, I decided to renovate the house and its contents. This included replacing the assorted dining room chairs with stylish new ones. The dining room chairs that most appealed in a local furniture store also came with a dining room table that also pressed the right buttons, so on impulse, we purchased the table along with the chairs.

Unfortunately, the quality of the new table precluded its acting as a support for the four boards of the prototype layout, so that has not been set up since. Furthermore, I have still not got round since to setting up the full-scale layout in either the spare bedroom or the third bedroom that acts as my office.

This was regrettable because even the prototype layout, which allowed me to run up to three locomotives simultaneously, served as a reminder of the steam trains I used to see and travel on. However, there was one significant threat. One of our pet cats got in the habit of ambushing the trains and de-railing them with a large paw from underneath the table.

Apart from a tortoise when I was very young, cats were the only animals I had any dealings with. When I was a child, we had two pet cats, but when Rosemary moved in with me, she brought two, Worzel and Merlin. After that, we have had a succession of cats, and at one stage, we had four. Generally, they were strays that appeared on the doorstep, but whatever their origins, I grew very fond of them all and found their presence very relaxing.

Like most pet owners, I found losing them extremely upsetting, a particular problem being the volume of traffic on Hazelbottom Road, which accounted for several of them. Fortunately, however, in recent years, we had introduced a regime whereby they steer clear of any contact with the road. Their veterinary needs were also of interest as well as being quite expensive.

This was especially true of three of them. Gerry Cat had been visiting our garden for some time when one day he appeared with a severe wound between his front leg and body. This refused to heal, even after stitches were applied. And so, our normal vet referred us to a specialist who had an international reputation in the treatment of small animal wounds. He performed an internal skin graft stretching skin from Gerry's stomach and stitching it underneath the wound. This procedure had a ninety percent success rate, but unfortunately, with Gerry it was only partially successful.

The wound did not heal, but the membrane that covered it seemed to prevent its getting infected, and Gerry lived happily with it subject to its being regularly cleaned by Rosemary. Then, after ten years, for no apparent reason and to the amazement of the vets, it miraculously healed totally in a matter of weeks.

Dilly (Delilah) Cat was a beautiful long-haired tortoiseshell who reminded me of the lady cat who sat on top of dustbins combing her hair with a fishbone in Tom and Gerry cartoons. At the age of approximately sixteen, she developed a cancerous lump on one of her back legs. She was referred to another vet who specialised in animal cancers. His treatment was to radiate the lump in a way that made it receptive to ointments. The treatment delayed the cancer, and Dilly lived for nearly another three years.

She was accompanied by her two brothers, Sammy and Titus, who both had long hair like a ruff around their necks resembling choir boys. Unfortunately, neither of them were with us long, succumbing to the Hazelbottom Road traffic.

Katie Cat was white with tortoiseshell markings. Like Gerry, she was a stray who adopted us. Despite having many medical problems, she had a delightful personality and would almost talk to you. Her principal medical problem in later years was diabetes which required insulin injections twice daily and periodic testing of her blood sugar level, all of which she stoically put up with. She has just passed away naturally and is sorely missed.

Amongst the other cats was Charlie, a ginger who was so clever he could open the fridge door, but his cleverness did not stop him becoming another victim, at an early age, of the traffic on Hazelbottom Road.

The most laid back was Top Cat (TC), another male tabby, whilst arguably the most anti-social was Olly. He was black with white markings, which reminded me of a waiter in a posh restaurant, and he started life as Holly until we took her/him to be neutered.

Like humans, I find their different personalities fascinating, but unlike humans, I am, of course, unable to ascertain what they are thinking, which I find somewhat frustrating.

The last three cats – Dilly, Gerry and Kate.

CHAPTER 31

IN CONCLUSION

I was lucky enough to be born intellectually very bright. Although physically and health-wise not so robust, this has not distracted from me capitalising on this innate brightness. Obviously, I have not always reached the full potential that could be expected from one so gifted. This was particularly so of my undergraduate years, but on reflection, I cannot say this has particularly held me back.

Another advantage I have enjoyed is that not having married and had children has enabled me to largely concentrate on work and my career. This is, of course, a double-edged sword in that I have missed out on the benefits that marriage and children would have brought me.

Additional to the concentration factor, the absence of needing to provide for a family had the added benefit that I was not so dependent on a particular employer and or job, so I could up sticks whenever I was unhappy in a particular organisation. The buoyant employment market for IT personnel during all the years I was working, of course, facilitated this.

The final step in this was, of course, setting up my own company. However, I put down this "restlessness" to a perhaps over idealistic view of how things should be with my father's abhorrence of lies somewhere in the background. Working in IT and perhaps engineering generally with their requirements for exactitude at the detailed level were perhaps also factors.

Throughout the moves in my career, there was no pre-planned strategy. At School, until I realised where my potential was, I was not overly ambitious, over and above, for what a working-class boy would consider as a good job. It was my headmaster at North Manchester who pointed out when I stated I wanted to be a draughtsman that my potential was much higher.

However, I gradually had the feeling that I would accomplish great things. The latter was manifest particularly when I looked on the Houses of Parliament as a student crossing Waterloo Bridge on my way to Kings. This is not to say I ever, apart from a few fleeting moments, contemplated a career in politics.

Some people seem to map out their future, and everything they do is geared to this, whereas not only did I not have a long-term plan, but as recounted previously, it was during my time with the Civil Aviation Authority that I made the decision that my own career interests would be subordinate to doing what I considered right and ethical.

Although I did not have any over-arching long-term career plan, this is not to say that I did not have plans for each section of my career with each employer. These plans, as the previous chapters have described, generally were self-conceived and innovative.

The notable exception was, of course, the Sheffield University Maxi Projects, the strategic concept of which belonged to others. Obviously, there was an element of luck in my being able to progress the innovations I conceived in that a variety of circumstances meant my superiors gave me the space to carry them out. However, this, too, was again a double-edged sword in that I never had a mentor or sponsor to support my stratagems. I guess that I must therefore have had a degree of self-confidence to operate without such support.

Considering my working-class background and where I have been, I am obviously an example of upward social mobility. I have joked that I was not born with a silver spoon in my mouth but rammed one there as soon as was possible. Nevertheless, I was never conscious of being fazed as I moved upwards, although, at times, I was not as pushy as I might have been. Perhaps, I have lived in my own bubble, oblivious to a degree to the world outside. This maybe has enabled me to return, with relative equilibrium in later life, to the impoverished surroundings where I grew up. That is not to say that sometimes whilst waiting for a local bus I do not wistfully remember when I was transported by executive jet.

Some traits did, however, linger from my roots. For many years, I did no long-term financial planning and money-wise lived from salary cheque to salary cheque. It was only in middle age, with the purchase and sale of my London Flat and then the need to set up a company pension scheme, that I started to consider my financial future. As a result, over my career, I have probably been under financially rewarded, compared to what I could have expected.

That is not to say that I am not reasonably well off in retirement.

What my career has done is given me, I believe, a wide spread of experience across sectors of society. This is not only across classes but across organisational sectors, including public and private, as well as academia and the media. Also, my non-career activities with the Church and in the community have given me insights into the former and local government. Working in the USA and Europe as well as the UK has further broadened my experience.

The overriding conclusion this has given me is that mankind in one respect has not advanced and is divided into tribes. These are not, however, the tribes of prehistoric times separated from each other by geography, although such tribes still exist but are tribes based on, for example, professions.

This means that society is driven by misconceptions about a particular tribe from outside the tribe. For example, some academics consider those in commerce and industry to be relatively overpaid with sumptuous expense accounts. In contrast, some of the latter consider the former to have a relatively stress-free existence with constant travel to conferences in often exotic locations. Also, within the tribes, groupthink often prevails.

My observations also include that some tribes practices are more closely associated with another tribe's practices than is generally assumed. For example, big business has perhaps more in common with public sector organisations than it has with small and medium-sized enterprises. That said, I often described relations between the public sector Civil Aviation Authority and IBM, as Godzilla meets the Black Swamp.

There is another phenomenon that I have seen constantly, both in my general work and specifically in the monitoring work. This is the ability of people to be self-delusional. This is particularly so when it comes to the slippage of timescales. Often I have visited a project, and they declare they are so many weeks or months late. Then visiting them say a quarter later, they say they have slipped so many weeks or months late. I then have to ask, "is this the total slippage" but frequently, it transpires that it is new slippage and the total slippage is this new plus the previous slippage. To me, this is an indication that short-terminism bedevils society and which, coupled to the tribalism, makes for a relatively unreal world. This unreality is further exacerbated when information is condensed into headlines and now simplistic tweets.

My intellect and my broad spread of experience have, I believe, given me the ability to see through the self-delusional unreality and groupthink which is endemic throughout most of society. Indeed although not quite the same, albeit related, one friend and colleague occupying a senior position once remarked that I was a prophet.

During the latter years of my career, confronting whilst not offending those afflicted with unreality is one of the hardest tasks I have undertaken. Composing words both spoken and written to facilitate this has occupied a significant amount of my time and mental effort. However, the fact that I have largely achieved it without making too many enemies tends to persuade me that in this respect, my career and possibly my life is a success.

This, of course, is possibly arrogance, along with the assumption that the ideas that I have tried to get across are valid.

Stan Price

PROJECTS MONITORED

	Name/Period/ Programme Budget	Partners	Topic
1	SIMMER 1986-1989 Alvey Programme	Edinburgh University International Computers Ltd (ICL) British Telecom (BT)	Integrated Modelling Support Environment
2	Software Data Library 1986-1989 Alvey Programme	National Computing Centre ICL Logica Cambridge and Others	Creation and Population of a Database of Software Development Metrics
3	ASDG 1987-1991 Alvey Programme	University of Ulster (Hull)	Automated System Generator
4	DREAM 1990-1993	York University (Monk) Data Logic System Concepts	Deriving and Representing Application Models

	Name/Period/ Programme Budget	Partners	Topic
5	VAR 1990-1993 Information Engineering Advanced Technology Programme (IEATP) £1,078,727	University of Surrey (Kittler) University of York (Hancock) Defence Research Agency British Aerospace Rutherford Appleton Laboratories.	Vision by Associative Reasoning
6	CONCENSUS 1990-1993 IEATP	Durham University (Slade) Cambridge Consultants British Aerospace	Methodological Issues in the Design of Parallel Knowledge-Based Co-operating Systems
7	EDISIRL 1990-1994 IEATP £929,724	University of Salford (Brandon) Royal Institute of Chartered Surveyors (RICS) Imaginor Systems Inference (Europe) Ltd.	Evolutionary Development of KBS in a Real Life Environment
8	PUNS 1990-1993 IEATP	Strathclyde University (MacCallum) West Worcester Water Works Pro-Aqua Systems	Planning for Uncertainty

	Name/Period/ Programme Budget	Partners	Topic
9	INTEGRATED SCHEDULING SYSTEM 1990-1993 IEATP £810,138	Reading University (Addis) GEC Semiconductors Integrated Solutions Ltd	The Practical Integration of a Knowledge-Based Scheduling System with a Semiconductor Manufacturing System
10	Project Abandoned		
11	SAMSON 1991-1994 IEATP £991,595	Open University (Demaid) Queens Belfast (Smith) University of Ulster (Hughes) Shorts Brothers Lucas Ceramic Developments Expert Information Systems	Object-oriented approaches to materials selection in the engineering design process
12	FLASH 1991-1994 IEATP £890,261	Silsoe Research Institute Phillips Research Laboratories Lloyds Register	Handling, using AI, of malfunctioning sensors in real time system

	Name/Period/ Programme Budget	Partners	Topic
13	IMAGEN 1992-1995 IEATP £1,036,079	University of Sussex (Grimsdale) Link Miles Defence Research Agency	Knowledge- Based Modelling for Three- Dimensional Sciences
14	MORSE 1992-1995 Safety Critical Programme £2,342,742	University of Cambridge (Pulman) Lloyds Register West Middlesex Hospital Transmitton Dowty Controls British Aerospace Airbus	A Method for Object Re-Use in Safety Critical Environments
15	SAFESYS 1992-1993 Safety Critical Programme Budget – Not expended	EDS-Scicon Lloyds Register	Formation of an Experience Learning Club to Sponsor Safety Critical System Projects
16	SPAM 1994-1998 Safety Critical Programme £1,189,678	Security Reliability Consultants Gerrard Software	Investigating Security Paradigms Validity for Safety Critical Environments

	Name/Period/ Programme Budget	Partners	Topic
17	PRICES 1994-1999 Safety Critical Programme £1,030,252	Open University (Hall) City University (Carson) Lloyds Register Rolls- Royce Bae SEMA G P Elliot Electronic Systems Analysis Consultants	Productivity, Integrity & Capability Enhancement for Software. Human Factors in Safety Critical Systems Development
18	SYCOMPT 1994-1997 Computer Supported Cooperative Work (CSCW) Programme £1,622,900	Lancaster University (Rodden) NatWest Bank DEC Synchro Ltd	Systems Development & Cooperative Work: Methods & Techniques
19	ADEPT 1994-1997 Intelligent Systems Integration (ISIP) Programme £2,215,143	Queen Mary College, University of London (Jennings) Loughborough University (Alty) Cable & Wireless Nortel. Anite Systems ICI	Advanced Decision Environment for Process Tasks

	Name/Period/ Programme Budget	Partners	Topic
20	CHRONOS 1994-1997 ISIP Programme £1,606,838	Imperial College (Richards) UMIST (Theodoulidis) Lloyds Register of Shipping ICL	Scheduling using Artificial Intelligence
21	ARMAN 1995-1998 HPIP Programme £918,815	Queen Mary Westfield College (Cosmas) BNR Europe Ltd Cray Communications Ltd	Algorithms for control and management of Resources in ATM networks
22	DCAN 1995-1998 High Performance & Protocols (HPIP) Programme £964,400	University of Cambridge (Leslie) Architecture Projects Management Nemesys Research Ltd	Distributed Control of ATM Networks
23	BATMAN 1995-1998 HPIP Programme	University of Durham (Mellor) Nine Tiles Computer Systems CASE	Investigate Architectures for an ATM stream relay

	Name/Period/ Programme Budget	Partners	Topic
24	E-scape 1997 Creativity Award £44,700	Magnetic Media Ltd	Science learning for children using multi-media
25	Francois Actuel 1997-1998 Creativity Award Budget Unknown	CD Live Ltd	CD with French Media extracts for learning French
26	Soundpad 1997 Creativity Award £97,600	Media Spec UK Ltd	Portable digital news-gathering device
27	Active Text 1997-1998 Creativity Award Budget Unknown	Abbey Information Systems	
28	24 Hour Box Office 1998 Creativity Award £43,868	Dataculture Ltd	Telephone & Internet ticket sales with on-site collection kiosk
29	Glowworm 1998 Creativity Award Budget Unknown £98,200	Realize	Search Engine using sophisticated parsing

Name/Period/ Programme Budget	Partners	Topic
30	Coping With Life 1998 Creativity Award	SMS Multimedia Consultancy	CD with interactive media for help with coping, initially bullying
31	Script to Screen 1998 Creativity Award	Mersey TV	
32 - 39	Unused		
40	CENTRE for 3D ELECTRONIC COMMERCE Comprises 41-44 Below	University College London (Treleaven) Participant in all of 41 – 44 Below	
41	Customer Clothing 1999-2001 £380.882 Actual	De Montfort University [Harwood] Hobsons & Sons [London] Ltd Ministry of Defence [MOD], Defence Clothing & Textiles Agency [DCTA] Gieves and Hawkes, British Airways CAD for CAD	A working made-to-measure clothing service from 2D/3D body scanning to manufacture

	Name/Period/ Programme Budget	Partners	Topic
42	National Sizing Survey 1999-2002 £2,378,372 Actual	**Retailers** Arcadia Group plc, Debenhams plc, Freemans Grattan Home Shopping Ltd Great Universal Stores plc House of Fraser plc, John Lewis Partnership Littlewoods Retail Limited, Marks & Spencer plc Monsoon, N Brown Group plc, Oasis Stores Plc Redcats (UK), Rohan Designs Speedo International Ltd, Tesco Stores Ltd **Academic Institutions/ Contractors** London College of Fashion (Bougard) Nottingham Trent University Heriot-Watt University, School of Textiles Southampton Institute Leeds College of Art & Design Manchester Metropolitan University University of Central England University of Wales Institute, Cardiff Select Research, Smart Safety Gear Ltd Bodymetrics	Scanning of 10,000 UK men and women to survey size of adults over the full demographic spread

	Name/Period/ Programme Budget	Partners	Topic
43	Virtual Shopping 1999-2001 £199,404 Actual	Freemans Royal National Institute for the Blind [RNIB] National Cash Register (NCR), Videonetworks	Design and implementation of an interactive system for clothing selection and body fitting
44	Infrastructure Technologies 1999-2001 £98,085 Actual	Hamamatsu Photonics UK Ministry of Defence [MOD], Defence Clothing & Textiles Agency [DCTA]	Research into the Infrastructure required for the rest of Project 40
45	STOVES 2000-2003 £333,658	Liverpool University (Leng) Euro-Serv Stoves plc N A Software Ltd	Laptop tool for maintenance technicians
46	BROADBAND 2002-2006 PACCIT Programme £901,501	Goldsmiths College (Lash) Nottingham Trent University Hildebrand Interactive Ltd Archangel Filmworks Ltd Videonetworks/ Home Choice	Investigating the process of inter-firm technology and media alliances in the making of interactive programming

	Name/Period/ Programme Budget	Partners	Topic
47	EDRAMA 2003-2006 PACCIT Programme £838,901	Birmingham University (Barden) Maverick TV Ltd. BT Exact Hi8US Projects Ltd	Enhancing Direction & Monitoring Functions of Existing E-drama package using AI Introducing Emotion detection
48	CMIS 2006-2008 Technology Programme £802,447	University of Reading (Guy & Clements-Croome) Ove Arup Partners International. Thales Research & Technology (UK) Ltd.	Intelligent systems for the control of the building environment
49	INTERNET-ENABLED 2006-2008 Technology Programme £952,800	Strathclyde University (Clarke) Persimmons Homes plc Dundee City Council. Laing O'Rourke Scotland Ltd. Mitchell & Butlers Ayrshire Housing Building Research Association Ltd. Adam Communication Systems International.	Distant control of the utilities of various types of building via the internet

	Name/Period/ Programme Budget	Partners	Topic
50	PhysVis 2006-2010 Technology Programme £399,473	Innoval Technology Ltd SimX Ltd The Advanced Composite Group Ltd	Affordable, High-Performance Physics-Based Visualisation and Simulation of Complex Systems
51	Grapeshot 2006-2010 Technology Programme £312,027	Grapeshot Ltd IBM UK Ltd.	Visualising the Velocity and Distribution of Information Flows as Information is Published
52	Geomerics 2006-2008 Technology Programme £496,740	Cambridge University Geomerics Ltd.	New Visualisation and Compression Technologies for Animation
53	VORTIX 2006-2007 Technology Programme £421,359	Imperial College Transport for London Kizoom Software Ltd	Visualisation of Transport Interchanges in Real Time
55	ICECOM 2007-2009 Technology Programme £1,044,593	Loughborough University (Singh) PERA Innovation Ltd Inty Ltd Fortium ICA Ltd Essential Computing Ltd EEMA	Corporate Data Retrieval, Storage and Analysis

	Name/Period/ Programme Budget	Partners	Topic
56	TRU-EP 2007-2010 Intelligent Transport Systems & Services (ITSS) Programme £2,898,129	Trakm8 Ltd Omitec Ltd	Vehicle Telematics
57	3GRSE 2007-2009 ITSS Programme £809,639	Telnet Technology Services Ltd Citysync Ltd Efkon Road Pricing Ltd Transport Research Laboratory Ltd Traffic Signals UK Ltd	Converging Road Charging Devices with Traffic Signalling
58	Did not proceed		
59	CLASSAC 2008-2010 ITSS Programme £460,651	York University (Austin) PIPPS Technology Ltd	Developing number plate recognition camera classifying vehicle types in real time
60	The Trusted Driver Model for Privacy & Accountability 2007-2009 ITSS Programme £532,437	Kizoom Software Ltd Acute Technology Ltd DSP Design Ltd.	Providing Privacy and Reliability in Road Charging

	Name/Period/ Programme Budget	Partners	Topic
61	OCCUTEK 2008-2010 ITSS Programme £621,428	Lancaster University (Honary) HW Communications Ltd Autotxt Ltd.	Identification and application of vehicle occupancy levels

THE FORTY YEARS WAR
— STAN PRICE V IT

Lancaster University Presentation

PRICE PROJECT SERVICES LTD

- ## **Software Project Headlines Circa 1984**

Software Project Headlines
Circa 2000- 2004

- International (*even in space*)

- Cross- Sectors.

- Data Processing and Engineering.

- Private as well as Public Sector.

IGNORE False Prophets with Silver Bullets.

With acknowledgement to NBCUniversal

With acknowledgement to BBC

Stan Price

Printed in Great Britain
by Amazon

72564045R00167